PRAISE FOR A CULTURALLY PROFICIENT RESPONSE TO LGBT COMMUNITIES

"A Culturally Proficient Response to LGBT Communities is one of the most authentic books I have ever read on how to be more inclusive and equitable to the LGBT school community. The reflection, dialogue, and going deeper sections provide educators with the opportunity to do the inside-outside work necessary to be a culturally proficient educator inclusive of LGBT colleagues, students, and parents/community members. This book contains numerous practical applications written in the context of the cultural proficiency framework, guiding principles, tools, and continuum that make it immediately applicable and user friendly for schools."

**Tracey DuEst, Diversity and
Inclusion Consultant**
Cincinnati, OH

"With the goal of genuine inclusion and equity for the LGBTQ community, this is a timely and superbly written book for educational leaders striving to support personal transformation and social change in their schools and beyond."

Chris Brown, Assistant Professor
Brandon University, Manitoba, Canada

"Cultural competence as a construct requires a commitment to address more than race, ethnicity, gender, disability and socioeconomics. LGBTQ students are often bullied or excluded, are statistically over-represented among teen suicides, and have lower graduation rates overall. Because of fear, shame, and peer pressure, they often suffer in silence. The needs of these students are often overlooked because educators are unaware, uncomfortable, or poorly informed. The culturally competent school is proactive in its awareness of the needs of these students, its willingness to intervene, and its skills in working with LGBTQ issues."

**Nicelma King, Youth and Family
Development Specialist**
University of California, Davis

"Culturally proficient persons are urgently needed who will take the initiative to change prejudicial beliefs and educational practices, biased interactions, discrimination, or bullying directed toward anyone in the LGBT or broader community. This text enhances the critical reflection, will, and skills needed to help make cultural democracy a reality for all."

**John Robert Browne II, Education Consultant
and author of *Walking the Equity Talk***
San Diego, CA

"LGBT students want to be respected and understood as individuals; not just as a member of a demographic group or other impersonal category. Our schools and districts should be a safe, healthy, secure and inclusive environment for all employees and students. We need to ensure that there is a teacher in every classroom who cares that ALL students are treated with respect."

Jeff Chancer, Superintendent
Oxnard School District, CA

"The authors of this text apply their proven expertise of the deeply relational notions of Cultural Proficiency to the needs of school children marginalized by homophobia and heterosexism. Discussions of sexual orientation and gender identity are only rarely and controversially included in educational discourse, even while students such as Zac—quoted in the book's introduction—notes that, 'I did not feel safe in my own school, a place where I am supposed to be able to be myself and learn who I am.' In this text, the authors make it absolutely clear that school is the place for addressing issues of equity and for advancing a more generous and accepting society. Most of us have seen messages from the It Gets Better campaign, a project designed to bring attention and commitment to providing hope for lesbian, gay, transgender, bisexual and other bullied human beings. In this inspiring text the authors show how it gets better. And just as importantly, they explain why it must get better—because, according to Zac, the bigotry and intolerance 'hurt me and it hurts everyone.'"

Sheri Leafgren, Associate Professor
Miami University, OH

A Culturally Proficient Response to LGBT Communities

A Guide for Educators

Randall B. Lindsey

Richard M. Diaz

Kikanza Nuri-Robins

Raymond D. Terrell

Delores B. Lindsey

CORWIN
A SAGE Company

CORWIN
A SAGE Company

FOR INFORMATION:

Corwin

A SAGE Company

2455 Teller Road

Thousand Oaks, California 91320

(800) 233-9936

www.corwin.com

SAGE Publications Ltd.

1 Oliver's Yard

55 City Road

London EC1Y 1SP

United Kingdom

SAGE Publications India Pvt. Ltd.

B 1/I 1 Mohan Cooperative Industrial Area

Mathura Road, New Delhi 110 044

India

SAGE Publications Asia-Pacific Pte. Ltd.

3 Church Street

#10-04 Samsung Hub

Singapore 049483

Acquisitions Editor: Dan Alpert

Associate Editor: Kimberly Greenberg

Editorial Assistant: Heidi Arndt

Production Editor: Amy Schroller

Copy Editor: Linda Gray

Typesetter: C&M Digitals (P) Ltd.

Proofreader: Jennifer Thompson

Indexer: Judy Hunt

Cover Designer: Michael Dubowe

Permissions Editor: Karen Ehrmann

Copyright © 2013 by Randall B. Lindsey, Richard M. Diaz, Kikanza J. Nuri-Robins, Raymond D. Terrell, and Delores B. Lindsey

Printed in the United States of America

A catalog record of this book is available from the Library of Congress.

ISBN 978-1-4522-4198-2

This book is printed on acid-free paper.

SUSTAINABLE FORESTRY INITIATIVE
Certified Chain of Custody
Promoting Sustainable Forestry
www.sfiprogram.org
SFI-01268
SFI label applies to text stock

13 14 15 16 17 10 9 8 7 6 5 4 3 2 1

Contents

Foreword   viii
Timothy Kaltenecker, EdD

Acknowledgments   x

About the Authors   xii

Introduction   1

PART I. Introduction: Background, Challenges, and Opportunity   7

1. Context   9
     Getting Centered   9
     Sexual Orientation as an Equity Issue   10
     Our Language: An Equity Indicator   11
     Range of Sexual Differences and Associated Terminology   13
     The Tools of Cultural Proficiency   16
     Going Deeper   17

2. The Tools of Cultural Proficiency   19
     Getting Centered   19
     The Conceptual Framework Is a Guide   22
     Transforming the Culture of School   26
     Levels of Commitment to Change and Improvement   27
     Culturally Proficient Leadership Links Behaviors
         With Beliefs and Identity   31
     Going Deeper   32

3. Equality and Equity Are Both Important, Just Not the Same   35
     Getting Centered   35
     Historical Bases for Equality and Equity   36
     Changing the Context   41
     Going Deeper   43

4. **Understanding Our History Helps Shape Our Future**   45
   Getting Centered   45
   North American Exceptionalism: Emergent Civil
      and Human Rights   47
   Activity   50
   Historical Perspective   51
   Heterosexism and Human Rights   52
   The Tools of Cultural Proficiency Frame Challenges and
      Opportunities   53
   Going Deeper   54
   Suggested Further Reading   55

PART II. Westfield Unified School District   57

5. **Creating Safe Space: Moving From Compliance to Advocacy**   60
   Getting Centered   60
   What Is Bullying?   61
   Why Do People Bully?   62
   Current Data on Bullying   63
   Two-Phase Response to Bullying   65
   Going Deeper   70

6. **Assessing Cultural Knowledge**   72
   Getting Centered   72
   Assessing Cultural Knowledge   73
   Listen to Self   79
   Going Deeper   79

7. **Valuing Diversity**   82
   Getting Centered   82
   Westfield Unified School District Case Story   86
   Going Deeper   88

8. **Managing the Dynamics of Difference**   91
   Getting Centered   91
   Westfield Unified School District Case Story   92
   Religion   94
   Bullying Targets   95
   Targets and Micro-Aggressions and Micro-Assaults   95
   Manage Through Facilitation   98
   Going Deeper   99

9. **Adapting to Diversity**   100
   Getting Centered   100
   Adapting to Diversity Within the School Community   101

Westfield Unified School District Case Story   102
Adapting to Diversity   103
Going Deeper   106

**10. Institutionalizing Cultural Knowledge: You,
Your School, and Your Community**   **108**
Getting Centered   108
Institutionalizing Cultural Knowledge: An Inside-Out Process   109
My Inside-Out Learning Process   111
Westfield Unified School District Case Story   112
Professional Learning for General Educators   114
Going Deeper   115

PART III. Next Steps   **117**

11. Moving From Bystander to Ally   **118**
Being an Ally: The Inside-Out Process Begins With You   119
An Invitation   120
Conversations Matter   124

Why We Do This Work   **125**

Resources   **131**
Resource A.1: Book Study Guide   132
Resource A.2: The "Apps" of Cultural Proficiency   138
Resource B: Quick Glossary of Terms   139
Resource C.1: Sexual Orientation Questionnaire   140
Resource C.2: Unpacking the Knapsack of
    Sexual Orientation Privilege   143
Resource D: Community Resources: Justice and
    Equity for LGBT Communities   145
Resource E: Cultural Proficiency Books' Essential Questions   150

References and Further Readings   **156**

Index   **160**

Foreword

It was the summer of 1981, months before my final year of high school, when I first acknowledged my sexual orientation publicly to a group of friends and soon after to my family. The thought of returning to school in September frightened me, a return to the oppressed corridors of this small-town high school where the taunts, ridicule, and aggression echoed daily. Up to this point, my existence was a façade to all except the very few I let behind the curtain on that summer evening. I may never know all the factors that contributed to my ability to "come out" at that time, but I can say for sure that, in part, the supportive and loving adults in my life—namely, my parents and teachers—created the foundation that would give me confidence in all aspects of my identity. Despite the prevailing culture in the Midwest at this time, I was able to emerge with a positive self-image intact.

The school is a social system with structures and norms that embody the culture of the environment. The culture, commonly referred to as "the way we do things around here," is displayed in the attitudes, beliefs, and behaviors of the school community. It operates on autopilot. The social interactions and power relationships are clearly defined and reinforced regularly as we reward the expected behaviors. This is not all bad as the adults must maintain control of the school environment. But we make assumptions about the students in our classrooms and our colleagues with whom we work. I recall a conversation I had with a colleague early in my career. Toward the end of my first year, this teacher, who I was beginning to socialize with outside of school, said to me, "I think we have a positive climate toward gays and lesbians here, don't you?" My response was, "How do you know?" We cannot equate silence with acceptance. And we cannot make assumptions about our school environments, particularly about those who are the invisible minority—the LGBTQ students.

My journey with cultural proficiency began during the first training session with our administrative team. Our skilled facilitators engaged us in a storytelling simulation. I sat at a table with colleagues I'd worked with for over five years and learned more about their backgrounds in that one day than I did in all the time I'd worked with them. I heard stories that shed light on the ways people operate—what drives their interests, their motivations, and their interactions with others. It was the beginning of a growth trajectory that impacted me personally and professionally. It started with a simple task: Tell a story that reveals something about you that nobody knows.

It takes great force, a conscious effort on the part of skillful leaders, to redirect the momentum of the prevailing culture to one that is inclusive of everyone. In *A Culturally Proficient Response to LGBT Communities: A Guide for Educators* the authors offer guidance—a road map, if you will—to school leaders, teachers, and students to begin the journey of developing respectful schools for the invisible minority, for gay, lesbian, bisexual, transgender, and questioning members of our community. You can enter the map wherever you are in your voyage. For those new to exploring sexual orientation and gender identity, the authors provide the historical background and issues of equity and equality one needs to set the context for this important topic. If you are exploring cultural proficiency for the first time, the essential elements are explained through the lens of equity and diversity. The case study and reflective questions will help you connect the concepts in the cultural proficiency framework to your personal and professional life.

And the urgency could not be greater. Recent surveys of school climate indicate high incidents of bullying among LGBT youth, and many states are developing strict policies to protect all students from discrimination in schools. News headlines tell too many tragic stories of alienated young people who take their own lives. *A Culturally Proficient Response to LGBT Communities: A Guide for Educators* is not a quick-fix program; the authors acknowledge that no single curriculum can solve the issues of bullying and make the lives of LGBTQ students better overnight. I see this text as "beyond bullying." That is, the authors move us beyond a reactionary approach toward a model that addresses the complex relationships and interactions that occur in our schools to provide a proactive framework for how we view ourselves, one another, and the world around us.

The times we live in now are a far cry from 1981. The age of the Internet, *Glee,* and the U.S. Supreme Court's consideration of gay marriage might make the lives of our children easier than they were decades ago. But how do we know? Have we asked our students to tell us a story about themselves? And are we prepared to hear it?

For anyone striving to create positive school cultures and inclusion for everyone, *A Culturally Proficient Response to LGBT Communities: A Guide for Educators* should be your go-to guidebook. Begin your journey now. Our children need you!

Timothy Kaltenecker, EdD
Assistant Superintendent
Byram Hills Central School District
Armonk, New York

Acknowledgments

We are mindful and are grateful for the many people who have contributed to the completion of this book: the patient support and sacrifices of family, the contributions of professional colleagues, and the inspiration of friends. Our words here are to honor their support for this work.

For me, Randy, it has been a growth experience to conceptualize and compose this book with Richard, Kikanza, Raymond, and Delores. To be able to work with friends who are also professional colleagues is one of the treats of my life. Our collective work on issues and topics of social justice is now in its fourth decade, and this book provides the opportunity for us to use the print medium to teach what we preach. To be able to write with Delores continues to be one of the joys of my life.

For me, Richard, this represents another step in my journey. To be able to work with friends who are motivated by true compassion is an honor. For me to be able to share my journey in life with these friends and colleagues has been remarkable. Together I hope we are able to make others more aware of the need to speak up for the rights of all people in our community.

For me, Kikanza, this book represents what happens when people who care about each other and the same social justice issues work together. Individually, we have all made contributions in this field; it is an honor and a privilege to be part of a collective that speaks out for oppressed, disposed, marginalized, and our personal struggles and still engages with the communities from which we emerged. More frequently than I like, I am reminded of my own growing edges; it is both a comfort and a source of personal strength to be able to learn and grow among friends.

For me, Raymond, the production of this book has allowed me to reach deep within myself and examine if I really walk my social justice talk. Working with my four writing partners and discussing this work with practitioners, friends, and family has also provided me with greater understanding of how others view sexual orientation. I mostly became aware of how silent most people are on the topic and how that silence tends to make many members of the community invisible. Now is the time for all of us to stand up for justice for all of us.

For me, Delores, cowriting this book has been another learning journey. I continue to learn about myself as an educator and grow as a writer. My cowriters and I knew this was the right time to write this book. I thank them for their expertise, their willingness to share their experiences, and their patience with me as a learner. I greatly appreciate and acknowledge the many educators with whom we work (the composite case stories) who continue to confront issues of inequity and injustice on behalf of students and employees. They, students and educators, are the people for whom we do this work. Thanks always to my husband, Randy, for being my cowriter and best friend.

We appreciate the careful review of our manuscript provided by Rabbi Elliot Kukla. His first-person perspective informed this work in ways that support our journey to become effective educators.

Our colleagues at Corwin have and continue to support our work in deep, authentic ways. Dan Alpert, our acquisitions editor, continuously serves as "friend of the work of equity" and embodies the commitment to social justice we associate with Corwin. Appreciation goes to Heidi Arndt, editorial assistant, whose high levels of support, responsiveness, and resourcefulness make the publication process proceed smoothly.

Publisher's Acknowledgments

Corwin gratefully acknowledges the contributions of the following reviewers:

Charisza Santos
Graduate School of Education and Counseling
Lewis and Clark College, Portland, OR

Shaun Travers
Campus Diversity Officer and Director of UC San Diego LGBT Resource Center
University of California, San Diego, La Jolla, CA

About the Authors

Randall B. Lindsey, PhD, is emeritus professor, California State University, Los Angeles and has a practice centered on educational consulting and issues related to equity and access. Prior to higher education faculty roles, Randy served as a junior and senior high school history teacher, a district office administrator for school desegregation, and executive director of a nonprofit corporation. All of Randy's experiences have been in working with diverse populations, and his area of study is the behavior of white people in multicultural settings. It is his belief and experience that too often members of dominant groups are observers of cross-cultural issues rather than personally involved with them. He works with colleagues to design and implement programs for and with schools and community-based organizations to provide access and achievement.

Randy and his wife and frequent coauthor, Delores, are enjoying this phase of life as grandparents, as educators, and in support of just causes that extend the promises of democracy throughout society in authentic ways.

Richard M. Diaz, MSEd, is director of the Riordan Leadership Institute, a program of the Los Angeles Junior Chamber of Commerce. Richard helps train business professionals to become board members of nonprofit agencies in the Greater Los Angeles area. Through his work, Richard has assisted many nonprofits to bring in new and diverse leadership to their organizations. Richard also consults with local nonprofits and their boards. He assists boards to review their mission and vision. Richard began his career as an elementary and middle school teacher and later supervised student teachers for Immaculate Heart College. He is a world traveler and lives with his partner, Gerry, of 23 years.

Kikanza Nuri-Robins, EdD, MDiv, is an organizational development consultant based in Los Angeles. She helps her clients close the gap between what they say they are and what they actually do, focusing on leadership development, change management, cultural proficiency, and spirituality at work. Kikanza works in a variety of settings, including education, health care, criminal justice, and religion. She has spent most of her career teaching school or consulting with public school educators. www.TheRobins Group.org

Raymond D. Terrell, EdD, is emeritus professor, School of Education, Health and Society, Miami University in Oxford, Ohio. He also served as a professor of educational administration and as Dean of the School of Education at California State University, Los Angeles. He began his career as a public school teacher, principal, and assistant superintendent in the Princeton City School District in Ohio. He has more than 40 years of professional experience with diversity and equity issues in urban and suburban school districts. Ray lives in Cincinnati, Ohio, with his wife Eloise. They both enjoy reading, writing, traveling, and spoiling adopted grandchildren.

Delores B. Lindsey, PhD, is a recently retired associate professor from California State University, San Marcos. She has served as a middle grades and high school teacher, assistant principal, principal, and county office administrator. Her primary focus is developing culturally proficient leadership practices. Using the lens of Cultural Proficiency, Delores helps educational leaders examine organizations' policies and practices, as well as individual beliefs and values about cross-cultural communication. Her message to her audiences focuses on nurturing socially just educational practices, developing culturally proficient leadership practices, and using diversity as an asset and a resource. Delores facilitates educators to develop their own inquiry and action research. She relies on the power of story and storytelling to enhance learning experiences. She asks reflective questions and encourages group members to use questions as prompts for their organizational stories. Her favorite reflective questions are these: *Who are we? Are we who we say we are?*

This book is dedicated to

Dan Alpert

You are our coach, colleague, and friend.

Thank you for joining us, and often leading us, on our life's journey.

Introduction

This book is about relationships. Educators working together to better serve all learners and members of school communities can confront the complex issues facing us in today's schools. Margaret Wheatley (2002) reminds us,

> Relationships are all there is. Everything in the universe only exists because it is in relationship to everything else. Nothing exists in isolation. We have to stop pretending we are individuals who can go it alone. (p. 19)

Of the many topics facing educators today, creating safe and respectful educational spaces for members of LGBT communities has finally become a priority. As authors of this book, we present an approach built on beliefs and values of human dignity, democracy, and equity. We believe that by working together, valuing our diversity, and confronting inequities, we can create conditions for a culturally proficient education environment for LGBT and straight students and adults. Once again, we quote Margaret Wheatley,

> Truly connecting with another human being gives us joy. The circumstances that create this connection don't matter. (p. 19)

Sexual orientation and gender identity are topics that prompt passionate responses in people in schools and communities across the United States and Canada. In many school communities, considering topics that address *lesbian, gay, bisexual, transgender, sexual orientation, homophobia,* and *heterosexism* topics is met with fierce resistance and hostility. Why does information and conversation about sexual orientation and gender identity provoke such emotions? How do we, as educators, craft positive, inclusive responses to counter negative comments? How do we create schools and communities that serve the educational and social needs of our students, faculty and staff, and community members that are inclusive of sexual orientation and gender identity? These are the questions that guided the authors to write this book.

PURPOSE AND ASSUMPTIONS

The purpose of this book is to provide a guide for you by which hetero-sexual and homosexual students, faculty and staff, and community members are to be served equitably by our schools. In preparing this manuscript, we identified our assumptions that provided the basic threads for this book:

- All students, faculty and staff, and community members are to have full access to the educational community in ways that acknowledge their sexual orientation or gender identity.
- One's sexual orientation or gender identity is as normal as any other cultural or demographic characteristic one possesses.
- Schools' organizational culture (the way people behave around here) is an important medium through which individuals and their cultures, including sexual orientation, are valued.

Why This Book Is Needed

During the final stages of assembling this manuscript, we received our monthly e-newsletter from Jer's Vision in Ottawa, Canada. We include it here because this young person makes the case for this book and others like it:

Dear Randall:

My name is Zac Johnstone, and I am a Grade 12 student at Colonel By High School, in Ottawa, Ontario. I am also the leader of my school's SAFE club (Students Advocating For Equality) and a volunteer with Jer's Vision.

As one of the few openly gay students at my school, I have experienced bullying and homophobia. As such, I volunteer to help all students feel safer at school.

It is important for us to feel safe at school. I was once terrified to even come to school. When I decided to come out of the closet, it took me half a year to come up with the courage to tell my friends because I was afraid of how they would take it. My friends were and are amazing people who did not have an issue with my sexual orientation. However, they used slurs like "faggot" and "you're so gay" every day as part of their normal language, which made me afraid of how they would take my coming out. I recall opening up my Facebook page one day to see a picture of me defaced, by a couple of students at my school, with homophobic slurs like "fag" and "homo." I did not feel safe in my own school, a school known as one of the most accepting in the city, a place where I am supposed to be able to be myself and learn who I am. When I came out, I was lucky that they were supportive, but I know not everyone is as fortunate as me.

School should be a place where we all feel welcomed and accepted, a place where no one should have to go through bullying of any kind. It hurt me and it hurts everyone. This is why we need Jer's Vision. This organization promotes respect, diversity, and a positive space for everyone. They work toward the ultimate goal of true equality in our communities. Jer's Vision helps clubs like SAFE by giving us support, mentorship, and information that help us make our schools a better place to be.

With the help of Jer's Vision, my SAFE club has worked over the years to make our school better for everyone. Last year, we had a record of eight students at my school come out of the closet safely and this could not have happened without the assistance of Jer's Vision.

Right now, I am helping Jer's Vision to organize the upcoming bilingual Dare to Stand Out Conference in Ottawa on October 19. This conference will give youth like me the tools to make their school a bully-free place, ideas to raise awareness about equality, and help foster a culture of respect in schools.

Jer's Vision.org e-mail, October 3, 2012. JERSVISION

54 Somerset St. W, Suite 1 | Ottawa, Ontario K2P0H5 CA

E-mail: info@jersvision.org | http://jersvision.org | http://dayofpink.org

We wrote this book to illustrate that sexual orientation and gender identity are diversity, equity, and cultural topics needing to be included and addressed in our schools. Viewing sexual orientation and gender identity as cultural groups is about all of us, including our students, our fellow employees, and the diverse communities we serve. We all have a sexual orientation. Some of us are heterosexual while others of us are lesbian, gay, bisexual, or transgender. Sexual orientation and gender identity can no longer be unmentionable topics in our schools. So the genie is out of the bottle, and as responsible educators and citizens, we must address the educational needs of LGBT communities as we do other cultural groups in our communities.

The content for this book is situated within the context of a diverse U.S., Canadian, and world community that includes sexual orientation and gender identity as important, too often overlooked, and purposefully marginalized demographic groups. Sexual orientation and gender identity are often avoided topics, yet always present and rarely acknowledged in educational discourse. In our earlier works, we have repeatedly made reference to sexual orientation, homophobia, and heterosexism, but as authors, we have not addressed the systemic underpinnings that have historically marginalized, and continue to this day to marginalize, students, faculty, other school employees, and parents/guardians because of their sexual orientation or gender identity. We present in the Appendix how we, as authors, have grown to this place to be able to write this book. In doing so, in this volume we present a way for educators and members of their communities to learn and grow in ways that benefit all learners.

"PUSH BACKS" TO SEXUAL ORIENTATION AND GENDER IDENTITY

As Zac's letter implies, schools are complex cultural entities that reflect the communities in which schools are situated. Since 1964, schools in the United States, meaning the people who make up the organizations themselves, have had to make cultural changes in the manner in which they either resisted or embraced students because of their race, national origin, gender, special needs, and language acquisition while most often rendering sexual orientation and gender identity invisible. However, sexual orientation and gender identity have emerged as topics too long denied; they won't go away. Nor should they go away. There are three prevalent ways that schools and their communities try to derail confronting the inequities visited on lesbian, gay, bisexual, and transgender students, faculty and staff, and community members:

- Focusing on bullying as an issue too often dismissed as "kids will be kids"
- Relying on questionable theological arguments
- Presenting confusing and myopic personal views on homosexual orientation and gender identity by limiting focus to sexual activity, whereas heterosexual people are presented as more dynamic and multidimensional

Bullying and antibullying programs. Unfortunately, sexual orientation and gender identity have become identified with bullying. We say, *unfortunate* because the bullying of gay, lesbian, bisexual, and transgender students has surfaced the topics of sexual orientation and gender identity in ways that complicate informed discussion and decisions. Newspapers, magazines, and various forms of online media are constantly reporting instances of bullying and other forms of harassment that marginalize students, educators, and parents/guardians. Administrators, teachers, and counselors are well aware of the recent focus on bullying. Bullying and programs to help educators respond to bullying have taken center stage in school districts across the United States. Bullying is not new; bullying and harassment have been part of school classrooms and playgrounds all along. Why all of the sudden interest in bullying and bullying prevention programs in schools? To adequately answer the question of "Why now?" we must delve into underlying issues. To help us understand at a deeper level, exploring the question of the recent focus on bullying and antibullying programs may provide useful clues:

If bullying prevention programs are the answer, then what was the question?

We have experienced numerous antibullying programs that avoid the undiscussable topics of sexual orientation and gender identity. Such programs do not prepare adult participants for thoughtful, productive learning. Conversations that lead to personal and organizational cultural changes within schools confront and undercut the often unstated, silent permission to marginalize people because of their being lesbian, gay, bisexual, or transgender.

Theological arguments. The United States and Canada are countries that guarantee each person the right to worship and believe as he or she chooses. This guarantee embraces the widest array of beliefs and practices, including those who choose no religious or formal affiliation. The United States also separates church from government/state and, thereby, limits the exercise of one's beliefs in an educational setting if that person's beliefs infringe on another person's ability to be a fully functioning member of that community. The Canadian Charter of Rights and Freedom similarly guarantees equality before the law that specifically includes sexual orientation and gender identity. In other words, one person's religious rights do not take the place of another person's civil rights.

Myopic views of sexual orientation and gender identity. In our work with educators and staff, students, and community members, we often encounter people whose views on sexual orientation and gender identity are sometimes limited to hypersexuality. They seem to be incapable of viewing relationships whether heterosexual or LGBT as infinitely more complex than sexual liaisons. Healthy relationships are grounded in attraction that can lead to lasting and complex relationships, whether heterosexual or homosexual (Campos, 2005; Murray, 2000).

THE "INSIDE-OUT" PROCESS OF CHANGE

Cultural Proficiency is based in the notion that personal and organizational learning is an *inside-out* process (Cross, 1989). In our earlier works (Nuri-Robins, Lindsey, Lindsey, & Terrell, 2012; Terrell & Lindsey, 2009;

Lindsey, Nuri Robins, & Terrell, 2009; Lindsey, Roberts, & CampbellJones, 2005), we described and provided models for learning that are well received by teachers, leaders, and school district administrators and staff developers as well as university administrator and counselor preparation programs. This book adds to those works by providing the reader with a clear road map for learning as a personal journey.

In this book, we guide you to consider yourself within the context of the communities you serve. The book begins and ends with a focus on one's self with the premise that one cannot adequately lead change in schools or other organizations until one truly knows and understands oneself as a cultural entity and as an educator. The inside-out feature of Cultural Proficiency is an initial step in personal transformation and educational transformation. Cross (1989) and Campos (2005) in their seminal works locate school transformation as beginning with the recognition that for systemic change to occur it must, first, begin with how professionals view themselves in relation to the populations they serve.

In Part I, we initiate a discussion of equity and equality in our schools and related youth-serving organizations as a context for examining one's assumptions and beliefs about sexual orientation. We place particular emphasis on LGBT students, educators, and parents/guardians. The chapters in Part II guide use of the Essential Elements of Cultural Proficiency as a constructive means for creating personal and organizational change. The chapter in Part III is a guide in reflective and proactive use of the language and Tools of Cultural Proficiency for yourself and with your colleagues.

As the authors, we describe our own recognition and self-disclosure as an illustration of our inside-out growth processes, and in the Appendix we have included brief descriptions of how we came to write this book. Throughout the book, we use self-discovery processes of reflective journal writing and professional learning dialogic opportunities for the reader to locate, recognize, and eradicate internalized heterosexism and homophobia.

The Resources Section presents several aids to support your and your colleagues' professional learning. A book study guide is provided in Resource A.1 to guide your and your colleagues' examination of each chapter in this book. Resource A.2 is a depiction of the relationship of the Cultural Proficiency books to the original book, *Cultural Proficiency: A Manual for School Leaders*. Resource E presents the essential questions addressed by each of the cultural proficiency books. We commit these resources to you and your colleagues as you begin or continue your cultural proficiency journey.

Part I

Introduction

Background, Challenges, and Opportunity

Part I is intended to provide a background for responding to the questions, "Why do we need to address issues related to sexual orientation and gender diversity within the context of the school community?" and "How do we move forward?" Education in Canada and the United States has been on an increasingly upward trajectory of inclusiveness in the recent past. Responding to issues of sexual orientation and gender diversity in positive ways is an opportunity for creating a socially just society—certainly, an opportunity that is long overdue. Yes, we have yet to experience equality or true equity with regard to race, ethnicity, gender, national origin, or ableness; yet we can more forthrightly and authentically mitigate egregious practices against one of these cultural groups when we dare to confront practices of inequity toward all cultural groups—namely, LGBT members.

The chapters in Part I inform and support your knowledge of factors that impinge on equitable institutional practices that affect educators, students, and parents/guardians. The chapters are designed to discuss issues related to sexual orientation and gender diversity in ways that provide knowledge and skills for educators and schools striving to educate all students, heterosexual and homosexual. Educators who display inclusive practices ensure the likelihood of students living in socially just and democratic societies that seek to overcome oppression and marginalization.

- Chapter 1 introduces the historical context of sexual orientation and gender identity as equity issues, provides definitions of key terms used in the book, and begins the description of the Tools of Cultural Proficiency.

- Chapter 2 immerses the reader in an in-depth examination of the Tools of Cultural Proficiency as knowledge and skills to support your understanding of the moral nature of this work.
- Chapter 3 parses two important concepts—equality and equity. You will learn, or reinforce prior learning, how these terms support the processes and desired outcomes for socially just, democratic societies.
- Chapter 4 provides a historical perspective for sexual orientation and gender diversity valued in some cultures and vilified in others. The chapter amplifies the manner in which historical, systemic oppression has evolved to inform current discriminatory practices.

You are about to begin a personal journey of learning that will benefit you and the communities you serve.

1 Context

A moral imperative, that all students must be able to exist within inclusive school structures where they feel safe physically and psychologically, must be upheld because young people are required by law to attend school rather than having a choice.

—Linda K. Corbin (2011, p. 1)

GETTING CENTERED

Take a few minutes to think about and respond to the following questions:

- What terms would you use to describe your sexual orientation?
- To what extent have you ever thought about your having a sexual orientation?
- What might be some ways to describe your feelings when colleagues talk about their own gender identity and sexual orientation?
- What are your feelings as you read and respond to these questions?

Please use the following space to record your responses to these questions, your comments, and questions that you might have. Also take a moment to write how you felt while responding to these questions.

_____

_____

_____

_____

This chapter

- Introduces the historical nature of sexual orientation and gender identity inequity and equity as the context for understanding self within school roles of parent/guardian, student, or educator.
- Identifies and defines terms used to describe LGBT communities and presents nonoffensive language that can be used by educators. While many more terms are used to describe aspects of sexuality and sexual orientation, this list applies only to terms used in this book, which we believe you may find useful in conversations with your colleagues and community members.
- Provides an introduction to the Tools of Cultural Proficiency as a means of guiding personal and organizational actions that support access to equitable academic outcomes and extracurricular involvement for all students.

SEXUAL ORIENTATION AS AN EQUITY ISSUE

Lesbian, gay, bisexual, and transgender (LGBT) communities are too often viewed only in terms of perceived sexual behavior and rarely as cultural groups with norms and values that shape their lives. Confusion and misperceptions exist about who is in what is often referred to as the "LGBT" community. This book intends to counter and confront those issues by clarifying the importance of knowing and understanding these cultural groups as well as acknowledge the make-up of the several demographic groups within this highly diverse community.

Two of the authors were conducting a professional learning session with a group of educational leaders recently using *Culturally Proficient Leadership: The Personal Journey Begins Within* (Terrell & Lindsey, 2009). One of the activities invited participants to respond in writing to a series of prompts that included "Describe when you first became aware of your gender"; "Describe when you first became aware of your race and/or ethnicity"; "Describe when you first became aware of your social class"; and "Describe when you first became aware of your sexual orientation." Everyone was thoughtfully engaged in writing. We observed people thinking hard as evidenced by furrowed brows, sighs, giggles, and fierce writing. About twenty minutes into the activity, one of the participants asked in a very attentive and serious tone, "Ray and Randy, I don't know how to respond to the sexual orientation prompt. I am straight." Everyone sat upright in seeming stunned silence to see how we might respond. While we were measuring our response, one of his friends cut the awkward silence with, "Dude, straight *is* a sexual orientation." The participant flushed with mild embarrassment and everyone laughed aloud, somewhat nervously.

Though this experience offered a moment of levity, it also provided opportunity for a profound lesson. Sexual orientation is common to all humans. Sexual orientation and gender diversity are common throughout humanity (Murray, 2000). Left unspoken and unacknowledged, issues that arise from misconceptions about sexual orientation and gender identity foster discrimination, marginalization, and brutality toward LGBT students, family/community members, and educators. The civil rights energy unleashed in the 1960s has been slow to address sexual orientation and gender identity as equity issues in the manner that we acknowledge race, ethnicity, language acquisition, gender, social class, and special needs. Though equity has not been totally achieved in those areas, progress is being made, and one of the hallmarks of progress will be when we no longer single out the equity issues to be addressed in our schools.

We begin this journey of Cultural Proficiency by examining the language we use. Our words and phrases sometimes reveal underlying values and, at other times, awkward ignorance. Ignorance is not necessarily bad. At its core, ignorance is "not knowing." One of the basic tenets of Cultural Proficiency involves an "inside-out approach" to our learning, both personally and institutionally. By examining our language, we overcome our ignorance to become better informed and, in turn, can examine our values and behaviors in a manner that can lead to more authentic communication and problem solving with and in LGBT communities.

OUR LANGUAGE: AN EQUITY INDICATOR

How do "they" want to be addressed? is a common question posed by many beginning this journey. We can begin the journey by acknowledging that names and nicknames are extremely personal, almost sacred elements of many cultures. However, we also know that labels and categories complicate matters of identity even further. In moments of hesitation, we may ask ourselves, *Will I make a mistake if I use this term or that term?* Cross-cultural communications create consternation for many people. Epithets, insults, and charges of being politically correct abound in our schools across the continent. Our experience has been that two underlying dynamics add to miscommunication and misunderstandings:

- A lack of skill and confidence for being involved in cross-cultural communications
- A lack of will in the organizational culture, whether collective or collaborative groups, of many schools to promote mindful, cross-cultural communications

One of the purposes of this chapter is to clarify terms commonly associated with sexual orientation and gender identity as one way to develop new skills and confidence and build collaborative behaviors to work cross-culturally. In this section, we review terminology that, when mastered, equips you with information that may be new to you and, most important, will be accurate and will protect the integrity of all involved. Later in this chapter and in Chapter 3, equity is discussed as a concept that heightens the integrity of dominant and nondominant groups alike.

A prominent feature of this book is a case story developed in Chapters 6 through 10 that presents positive and constructive application of the Tools of Cultural Proficiency. In this opening chapter, characters from the case story are introduced in a brief vignette as a means to introduce concepts, social dynamics, and issues common in our schools and communities. Read the following short vignette and spend a few moments reflecting on the prompts that follow. As you proceed through the book you will learn that we rely on reflection and dialogue as means to internalize the information in ways that will be useful to you personally as an educator as well as being a member of a school learning community. The ensuing vignette introduces members of the Westfield Unified School District (WUSD) case story and provides a glimpse of some issues dealt with in Chapters 6 through 10. Sharon, Thomas, and Seth are teachers at one of the high schools in WUSD. They are leaving school one day and engage in the following conversation:

Story

Sharon: *I am not interested in learning about how homosexuals live.*

Thomas: *Yeah, before you know it, we are going to be decorating a float for gay pride day and, then, trying to keep our students from using the 3-letter "F" word.*

Sharon: *I think the word is gay. The PC police have excised one more perfectly good word from our "acceptable use" vocabulary. The "F" word is supposed to be as offensive as the "N" word.*

Seth: *Well, that is right. I couldn't help but overhear what you were saying. The professional development session we are having next week is supposed to help us.*

Thomas: *Help us! Are you kidding? Having a workshop on personal behavior that I find reprehensible and morally wrong is not going to help me to teach math.*

Seth: *No, it won't. So thank goodness that is not what the PD is about. We are going to learn how to work with our LGBT colleagues, students, and families.*

Sharon:	*Oh, you mean like Anna and Evelyn. Daniel told us what happened. He left a message for them the other day. When he called them, he said, "I know your child has two mothers, I would like the real parent to show up for the teacher conference."*
Seth:	*Yes, that's what I mean!*

Reflection

Take a few minutes to think about and respond to the following questions:

- If you were part of the conversation in the preceding section, what might you be thinking?
- What might you say? Why?
- What questions do you want to have answered in this chapter?
- Please use the space below to record your responses. Record your feelings that surfaced when reading this conversation.

_____

_____

_____

_____

RANGE OF SEXUAL DIFFERENCES AND ASSOCIATED TERMINOLOGY

Popular descriptions of sexuality are often in polar opposite terms—a person is male or female, gay or straight. However, the reality is that sexual orientation is more of a range along a line rather than a fixed, single point. The place range for some people might be very specific, often making it difficult to imagine an orientation other than theirs. The locale along the range of sexual orientation or gender identity for others may be quite long, which might ease their relating to people with different sexual orientations or gender identity.

Murray (2000), a highly respected authority of homosexuality from global and historical perspectives, notes that "no single type *homosexual* with a unique set of characteristics exists" (p. 1). He correctly observes that the same range of intracultural diversity exists within homosexual communities as there are within "Latino or Chinese or Italian, working-class or upper-class behaviors, typifications, self-identifications, and meanings" (p. 1).

Whether you are new to this discussion or a veteran well versed about the terms and issues that affect human sexual orientation and gender identity, we present key terms used throughout this book to support your reading. This chapter presents and defines those key terms. Resource B in the Appendix has terms that, though not all are part of this book, are germane to our ongoing learning about topics related to sexual orientation and gender diversity.

Key terms to inform your reading as you proceed through this book:

- **Culture:** Murray's (2000) contention that *"Culture" like "homosexuality" is an abstraction* appropriately frames discussions about humans organizing and creating groups across gender, racial, religious, social, and work identities (p. 8). A popular definition of culture, "the way we do things here," is an often-used, shorthand way to describe commonalities within categories of people. We use the term *culture* to refer to groupings of people with seemingly common characteristics, such as race, gender identity, sexual orientation, social class, ableness, and religious/faith/spirituality affiliation, among many others. It is the imprecision of use of the term culture that leads to the observation that there is as much diversity within cultures as there is among cultures. For our purpose, we persist in using the term culture in inclusive ways that frame the assets that exist among group members as opposed to the all-too-frequent function of stigmatizing the differences of "others" as deficits.

- **Sexual orientation:** "A person's emotional, physical, and sexual attraction to members of the opposite gender (heterosexual), same gender (gay or lesbian), or both (bisexual)" (Campos, 2005, p. 110).

- **Sexual identity:** The term a person uses to identify or describe his or her sexuality. One may identify as straight, gay, lesbian, bisexual, or transgender and one's sexual behavior may or may not be congruent with that person's sexual identity (Campos, 2005; Murray, 2000).

- **Gender identity:** "A person's self-perception or self-acceptance of being male, female, both or neither (androgynous)" (Campos, p. 107).

- **Homosexuals:** People attracted to members of their gender.

- **Heterosexuals**: People attracted to members of the opposite gender.

- **Gay**: Miller (2006) notes that the term *gay* is a fairly new term with many usages, emerging in the 1950s probably from the French word *gaie.* The term is most often used when describing homosexual men; however, it is sometimes used by lesbian, bisexual, and transgender people when describing themselves (p. 328).

- **Lesbian**: A term traced to ancient Greek history and the poet Sappho who lived on the island of Lesbos. It refers to homosexual women.

- **Transgender**: An umbrella term for many different gender identities. It can include anyone who sees himself or herself as a gender that is different from the gender he or she was assigned at birth. For example, a person may have been raised as a boy, but now sees herself as completely female or raised as a girl and now sees himself as completely male. Other transgender people may have an alternate gender identity that is neither male nor female, and for some people their gender identity may vary at different points in their lives. Some transgender people modify their bodies through medical means, such as hormones or surgeries, and some do not. These choices are highly individualized and influenced by medical, financial, and personal reasons and should not impact how much we see a person as a "real" man or a "real" woman. Gender identity is different from sexual orientation, and transgender people may identify as gay, straight, bisexual, queer, or have a fluid sexual orientation.

- **LGBTQ:** The Q is used for queer or questioning. The term *queer* has historically been used as an epithet against homosexuals, but now it is a term appropriated by many gay men and lesbians, as well as bisexual and transgender individuals to strongly affirm pride in their identity. The term *questioning* refers to people who are questioning their sexual orientation or identity and may, in time, identify as heterosexual, lesbian, gay, bisexual, or be in the process of becoming transgender (Campos, 2005; Webber, 2010).

- **Heterosexism**: The system of beliefs and practices that exclude and demean those who are, or are perceived to be, same-sex oriented. Heterosexism includes the promotion by individuals and/or institutions of the superiority of heterosexuality over all other orientations. Heterosexist beliefs include the assumption that everyone should be heterosexual and that everyone is heterosexual, unless known to be otherwise, and that non-heterosexuals are unnatural. Heterosexism can be intentional or unintentional. Heterosexist beliefs also refer to beliefs that lead people to invalidate the experiences intentionally or unintentionally of LGBT communities. Like other forms of discrimination, heterosexism is often invisible to those who are oblivious to discrimination or marginalization toward others. The belief that heterosexuality is a choice and is the appropriate choice to make and having the power to oppress or discriminate against those who do not make that choice is heterosexism.

- **Homophobia:** This term stems from the deep fear many heterosexuals have of sexual diversity. Homophobia is the term often used to describe personal forms of heterosexism, including verbal and physical abuse. Some find the roots of the term (the irrational fear of same-sex oriented people or feelings) useful in addressing heterosexist attitudes. However, others prefer to use the more inclusive term, *heterosexism*, to describe all forms of discrimination against lesbian, gay, bisexual, and transgender people.

- **Sexual preference:** A misnomer term used by people who assume that who one is attracted to is a choice. There is growing evidence that sexual orientation is an innate trait (Campos, 2005; Sullivan, 2008).

- **Lifestyle:** A misnomer often used to assume that homosexuality is chosen. Similar to sexual preference.

- **Internal language:** Refers to words and phrases that a community uses to address its own members. Sometimes words are used within a community that would be experienced as inflammatory, insulting, or hurtful if used by someone outside of the community. This use is confusing to outsiders who believe that if a word is inappropriate for one group to use, it should be inappropriate for all to use. However, this is a way that many cultures, especially nondominant groups, distinguish between members of their group and others. Think how family members address one another. They often use language that would be totally unacceptable coming from anyone outside the family unit. It is important therefore, not to use a term about a group because you have heard group members using it: Rather, one should err on the side of formality and ask how a person prefers to be addressed or described.

Sexual orientation, gender identity, and *sexual preference,* as you now know from our usage, are not interchangeable terms. For this reason, in this book, we use the terms sexual orientation and gender identity. Sexual orientation and gender identity are the preferred usage in LGBT communities and are terms that convey a person's sexuality. Resource B provides a quick glossary of words and terms that relate to LGBT communities.

THE TOOLS OF CULTURAL PROFICIENCY

An often-used phrase holds that "the ultimate power is the power to define." In absence of accurate information, stereotypes about people become the definitive perspective. Earlier we described and discussed terms that reveal what we know about sexual orientation and gender diversity and, often, our levels of comfort in talking about these topics. Knowledge can be increased with accurate information. Comfort can be heightened with accurate information coupled with a moral frame that values people for who they are rather than who you would like them to be.

The Tools of Cultural Proficiency provide a framework to guide examining personal values and behaviors and organizational policies and practices. As you read Chapter 2 about the Tools, you are guided in exploring an *inside-out* approach to change. Cross (1989) created this inside-out approach to personal and organizational change, and it has been the hallmark of each of our books on Cultural Proficiency. Now that you have an understanding of the terminology of sexual orientation, you will be able to use this book as a guide to becoming a more effective educator.

GOING DEEPER

Personal Reflection: Take a moment to think and respond to these questions:

- What questions do you still have about terminology or appropriate language in support of LGBT communities?
- Now that you have read this chapter, will you change any of your language?
- What would you like to share about what you have read and learned? If so, in what ways?
- With whom will you share it?

_____

_____

_____

_____

Dialogic Activity: Upon reading this chapter . . .

- What might be a learning initiative that you as a school staff want to undertake with regard to LGBT topics and issues?
- What might be your first steps?
- Who will take which responsibilities?
- In what ways will this book support your learning initiative?
- In what ways will you measure progress or success?

_____

_____

_____

_____

The journey to Cultural Proficiency is facilitated through the Tools referenced earlier in this chapter. In Chapter 2 you will learn about the Tools of Cultural Proficiency and the manner in which they support and facilitate your personal and organizational learning. The tools are these:

- Overcoming the Barriers to Cultural Proficiency: A description of how systemic oppression and a sense of privilege and entitlement foster resistance to change and an unawareness of our need to adapt, both of which limit our cross-cultural effectiveness
- Guiding Principles of Cultural Proficiency: A discussion of nine core values to inform our personal values and beliefs as well as our institutional policies and practices
- The Continuum: A six-point range of descriptors for behaviors, values, policies, and practices that illustrate the manner in which Barriers to Cultural Proficiency inform negative values/behaviors and policies/practices and how the Guiding Principles inform positive values/behaviors and policies/practices
- Essential Elements: Five standards of cultural competence used to craft effective personal/professional behaviors and school/institutional practices

2

The Tools of Cultural Proficiency

The genes lay down a range of possibilities, but your environment, your teaching, your education select among those possibilities.

—Philip Tobias (Dixon, 2012, p. AA6)

GETTING CENTERED

The epigraph that opens this chapter, from the obituary of renowned South African anthropologist Philip Tobias, expert on hominids and early man, describes his own intellect. That spirit of scanning our environments, being mindful of our teaching and leading, and continuing our education are centered in the Tools of Cultural Proficiency. These Tools along with this spirit of actively participating in our own learning enable us to become ever-effective educators in diverse and inclusive settings. Culturally proficient educators engage in personal reflection on their practice as well as become involved in cross-cultural dialogue with colleagues, students, and parents/guardians about shared educational and community interests. In our work with school districts across the United States and Canada, we have learned

---

AUTHORS' NOTE: For purposes of consistency, material in this chapter is adapted from earlier Cultural Proficiency books, most recently, Reyes L. Quezada, Delores B. Lindsey, & Randall B. Lindsey, *Culturally Proficient Practice: Supporting Educators of English Learning Students;* Randall B. Lindsey, Kikanza Nuri-Robins, & Raymond D. Terrell, *Cultural Proficiency: A Manual for School Leaders;* and, Delores B. Lindsey, Richard S. Martinez, & Randall B. Lindsey, *Culturally Proficient Coaching: Supporting Educators to Create Equitable Schools.*

that people and organizations who are effective in cross-cultural communication regularly engage in "thinking about their own thinking" and in "seeking to understand others"—two skills basic to Cultural Proficiency's inside-out approach to individual and organizational change.

Take a few minutes to think and respond to the following questions:

- What was your initial response to the phrase "personal reflection on practice"?
- What was your initial response to "cross-cultural dialogue with colleagues, students, and parents/guardians"?
- To what degree are you involved with your colleagues in conversations about educating all learners?
- What might be some ways in which you are engaged in thinking about your own learning?

_____

_____

_____

_____

Reflection and dialogue used in mindful and consistent ways are indispensable communication devices that support effective uses of the Tools of Cultural Proficiency. Schools are complex organizations made up of countless formal and informal communications networks. Our experiences have been that when educators intentionally and purposefully use reflection and dialogue, they contribute to healthy school environments for themselves and their students. The intersection of reflection and dialogue with Cultural Proficiency provides benefits:

- For individuals, the Tools of Cultural Proficiency guide reflection to recognize and understand barriers that impede your and your students' learning as well as core values that support and facilitate learning. Later in this chapter, we describe overcoming Barriers to Cultural Proficiency as critical to being an effective educator. Once barriers are evident to educators, continued reflective practice guides use of your and your students' cultural assets to sustain learning.

- For groups made up of any combination of teachers, administrators, counselors, trustee/board members, or any persons interested in educational issues, the Tools of Cultural Proficiency provide the opportunity for dialogue to lead to understanding individual and organizational cultures in the school. Similar to reflection, dialogue allows groups to recognize barriers to their and their students' learning and to purposefully embrace core values that view culture as assets, not deficits.

This intentional and purposeful combination of personal reflection and organizational dialogue leads to a healthy state we call the inside-out process of change. The focus of the change process is on shifting thinking and changing conversations from viewing culture as a deficiency to viewing culture as an asset.

Reflection and Dialogue Lead to Inside-Out Change

Culturally proficient practices, whether individual or organizational, are developed through intentional willingness to examine our own behavior and values as well as our school's (or district/board's) policies and practices. Examinations such as these are facilitated through the use of two communication devices referenced above—personal reflection and dialogue. Now that you have thought about and recorded your reaction to these two terms, let's take a look at how we believe these two communication techniques support your learning.

• *Reflection*—the conversation we have with ourselves that leads to even deeper understanding of our own values and beliefs. Sustained reflection often entails exploration of the cultural bases for one's belief systems and for "why" we do the things we do.

• *Dialogue*—the conversation we have with others to understand their values and beliefs. The emphasis is on understanding others and not on making decisions or solving problems or trying to convince others of the errors of their ways. Dialogue that explores organizational or institutional understanding seeks to explore the bases for stated policies and prevalent practices. Exploration into organizational policies and practices almost always finds that the initial reason given for current policies and practices is, "Well, it's always the way we have done it here." True, sustained dialogue seeks to go deeper to understand and explore the historical and/or cultural bases for policies and practices. The deeper dialogue helps members of the organization surface deeply held assumptions that have guided decisions and historically determined distribution of resources. Without exposing these assumptions, status quo continues without question or exposure. The questions, "Why do we do what we do?" and "Are we who we say we are?" are the ones that most often help surface long-held assumptions.

Educators who use the communication skills of reflection and dialogue to learn to apply the Tools of Cultural Proficiency are well positioned to provide effective high-level educational opportunities and outcomes to lesbian, gay, bisexual, and transgender (LGBT) students, educators, and parents/community members. In the hands of a skilled practitioner, the Tools of Cultural Proficiency enable you to intentionally change your practices and the policies and practices of your school in ways that better serve the educational needs of your LGBT communities and, in doing so, also serve dominant-group members in more authentic ways.

The Tools of Cultural Proficiency

The Tools of Cultural Proficiency enable you to do the following:

- Describe Barriers to Cultural Proficiency you may have experienced or observed that impede cultural proficiency
- Describe how the Guiding Principles of Cultural Proficiency serve as core values for your personal, professional, and organizational values and behavior
- Describe unhealthy and healthy values and behaviors and school policies and practices and plot them on the Cultural Proficiency Continuum
- Describe and use the five Essential Elements of Cultural Competence as standards for your personal and professional behavior and your school's formal policies and nonformal, prevalent practices.

THE CONCEPTUAL FRAMEWORK IS A GUIDE

The conceptual framework illustrates the manner in which cultural assets form the basis for core values to guide educational leaders. Recognizing and understanding the tension that exists for people and schools in terms of barriers versus assets, prepares you to better serve the students in your classroom, school, and district.

Table 2.1 (see pp. 24–25) presents the Conceptual Framework of Cultural Proficiency and shows the four Tools of Cultural Proficiency and the relationships among the Tools. Begin by reading Table 2.1 from the bottom up. Please regard reading in this fashion as a cultural experience.

Barriers Versus Cultural Assets: The Tension for Change

The Barriers to Cultural Proficiency and the Guiding Principles (e.g., core values) of Cultural Proficiency are the "invisible guiding hands" of the framework. Barriers inform the negative aspects of the Cultural Proficiency Continuum—Cultural Destructiveness, Cultural Incapacity, and Cultural Blindness—while the Guiding Principles serve to inform the positive aspects of the Cultural Proficiency Continuum—Cultural

Precompetence, Cultural Competence, and Cultural Proficiency. Being able to recognize and acknowledge the Barriers to Cultural Proficiency is basic to understanding how to overcome resistance to change within us and in our schools. From Table 2.1 you learned there are barriers to culturally proficient attitudes, behaviors, policies, and practices that affect our daily lives and impact educational leaders' decisions (Cross, 1989; Lindsey, Nuri-Robins, & Terrell, 1999, 2003, 2009):

- Being resistant to change
- Being unaware of the need to adapt
- Not acknowledging systemic oppression
- Benefiting from a sense of privilege and entitlement.

Notice the line between the Barriers and the Guiding Principles. That line extends between Cultural Blindness and Cultural Precompetence and represents the paradigmatic shifting point where educators have clearly delineated choices:

- To the left of the line people choose to be victims of social forces and to believe either in cultural deficit theory applied to LGBT communities or, every bit as damaging, the intractability of systemic oppression visited on LGBT communities.
- To the right of the line people choose to believe in their capacity to effectively educate LGBT students.

The Guiding Principles of Cultural Proficiency function as a counter to the Barriers to Cultural Proficiency by serving as core values in developing our capacity for personal and professional work that results in LGBT students being academically successful and full participants in the extracurricular programs of the school. Culture is inculcated in the Guiding Principles and can be readily seen in our behaviors, policies, and practices. Let us be direct and specific: To be effective, the core values must be deeply held beliefs and values. They cannot and must not be lightly agreed to in nodding assent and then blithely ignored. The Guiding Principles inform our actions for being Culturally Precompetent, Culturally Competent, and Culturally Proficient. The Guiding Principles follow here, continuing on p. 26:

- Culture is a predominant force in people's and schools' lives.
- People are served in varying degrees by the dominant culture.
- People have group identities and individual identities.
- Diversity within cultures is vast and significant.
- Each cultural group has unique cultural needs.
- The best of both worlds enhances the capacity of all.

Table 2.1 The Cultural Proficiency Framework

The Essential Elements					

Standards for Planning and Evaluating

- **Assess Culture:** Identify the cultural groups present in the system.
- **Value Diversity:** Develop an appreciation for the differences among and between groups.
- **Manage the Dynamics of Difference:** Learn to respond appropriately and effectively to the issues that arise in a diverse environment.
- **Adapt to Diversity:** Change and adopt new policies and practices that support diversity and inclusion.
- **Institutionalize Cultural Knowledge:** Drive the changes into the systems of the organization.

Cultural Proficiency Continuum

Change Mandated for Tolerance			*Change Chosen for Transformation*		
Destruction	**Incapacity**	**Blindness**	**Precompetence**	**Competence**	**Proficiency**
Eliminate differences.	*Demean differences.*	*Dismiss differences.*	*Respond inadequately to the dynamics of difference.*	*Engage with differences using the essential elements as standards.*	*Esteem and learn from differences as a lifelong practice.*
The elimination of other people's cultures	Belief in the superiority of one's culture and behavior that disempowers another's culture	Acting as if the cultural differences you see do not matter or not recognizing that there are differences among and between cultures	Awareness of the limitations of one's skills or an organization's practices when interacting with other cultural groups	Using the five essential elements of cultural proficiency as the standard for individual behavior and organizational practices	Knowing how to learn about and from individual and organizational culture; interacting effectively in a variety of cultural environments. Advocating for others

Reactive Behaviors, Shaped by the Barriers	Proactive Behaviors, Shaped by the Guiding Principles
• Unawareness of the need to adapt • Resistance to change • Systems of oppression and privilege • A sense of entitlement	• Culture is a predominant force in people's and schools' lives. • People are served in varying degrees by the dominant culture. • People have group identities and individual identities. • Diversity within cultures is vast and significant. • Each cultural group has unique cultural needs. • The best of both worlds enhances the capacity of all. • The family, as defined by each culture, is the primary system of support in the education of children. • School systems must recognize that marginalized populations have to be at least bicultural and that this status creates a unique set of issues to which the system must be equipped to respond. • Inherent in cross-cultural interactions are dynamics that must be acknowledged, adjusted to, and accepted.

Source: Adapted from Nuri-Robins, Lindsey, Lindsey, and Terrell. (2012). *Culturally Proficient Instruction: A Book for People Who Teach* (3rd ed.; Figure 1.1). Thousand Oaks, CA: Corwin.

- The family, as defined by each culture, is the primary system of support in the education of children.
- School systems must recognize that marginalized populations have to be at least bicultural and that this status creates a unique set of issues to which the system must be equipped to respond.
- Inherent in cross-cultural interactions are dynamics that must be acknowledged, adjusted to, and accepted.

TRANSFORMING THE CULTURE OF SCHOOL

Of all the cultural groups that schools serve, the organizational culture of school is the group that most often is the focus of "change, or needs to be changed." Organizational and school culture have been studied extensively even in recent years (Deal & Kennedy, 1982; Fullan, 2003; Schein, 1992, 2004, 2010; Wagner et al., 2006). Both veteran and new educators acknowledge that change is not easy. Within schools abide forces that either block (Barriers) or facilitate (Guiding Principles) student achievement. Implementing new practices in schools is often difficult and made even more difficult when issues serving the educational needs of LGBT students are embedded in change processes. In Chapter 1, we described the slowly evolving national context of a society responding to the educational needs of LGBT communities. Although it may be true that change is not easy, we know also that change is inevitable and natural. When properly understood and implemented, the change process can be led in ways that target the educational needs of LGBT students and, at the same time, benefit all learners in our schools.

Formal and nonformal school leaders must be able to recognize and acknowledge personal and institutional barriers to creating conditions for teaching and learning while advocating for practices that benefit all students, schools, and districts. The Conceptual Framework of Cultural Proficiency is a mental model for managing change that we use to understand and tell our stories in ways that may inform you as you continue your journey to increased effectiveness as an educator (Dilts, 1990, 1994; Lindsey, Nuri-Robins, & Terrell, 2009; Senge et al., 2012).

Regarding Culture as an Asset Leads to Cultural Proficiency

The Cultural Proficiency Continuum and Essential Elements of Cultural Proficiency are the visible Tools of Cultural Proficiency and are represented by what we do, not by what we say we do. The Essential Elements are standards for personal and professional behavior as well as for organizational policies and practices. As noted above, the Guiding Principles are core values that inform and guide the Essential Elements. When culture is embraced as an asset, educational successes can be crafted, both for ourselves as educators and for the communities we serve. Tables 2.2 and 2.3 describe in greater detail the phases of the Cultural Proficiency Continuum and the Essential Elements of Cultural Proficiency.

Table 2.2, The Cultural Proficiency Continuum: Depicting Unhealthy and Healthy Practices, aligns the six phases of Cultural Proficiency so you can see clearly that the Barriers to Cultural Proficiency inform Cultural Destructiveness, Cultural Incapacity, and Cultural Blindness. These phases are, at best, half-hearted compliance-driven behaviors that rarely result in actions to support the academic and social success of LGBT students or the effective inclusion of LGBT colleagues and community members. In marked contrast, the Guiding Principles of Cultural Proficiency serve as core values to support Culturally Precompetent, Culturally Competent, and Culturally Proficient behaviors, policies and practices for LGBT students, educators, and parents/community members by esteeming their cultures.

Table 2.3 displays The Essential Elements of Cultural Proficiency. This is the point on the Continuum "where the action is." Our caution to you is that blind adherence to these five standards without a full understanding of the Barriers and Guiding Principles will, most assuredly, lead to frustration. Being equipped with effective teaching and leadership strategies that honor and recognize LGBT communities combined with the view that our students' cultures are assets on which to build a relationship, you will be better prepared and less frustrated to meet the academic and social needs of LGBT students. Take a moment and study Table 2.3, The Essential Elements for Culturally Proficient Practices, and ask in what ways these "actions" can inform your practice.

LEVELS OF COMMITMENT TO CHANGE AND IMPROVEMENT

In this section, our discussion of large-scale change initiatives is adapted from a previously cited publication, *Culturally Proficient Coaching: Supporting Educators to Create Equitable Schools* (Lindsey, Martinez, & Lindsey, 2007). We reference this work here because the degree of commitment to a change initiative that a school or district holds is often the primary indicator of success or failure in reaching its student performance goals. The level of commitment is reflected in the educators' public rhetoric, the resources (i.e., inclusive of time, people, money, materials) assigned to the initiative, their widely held beliefs that the initiative can produce desired results, the overall efforts to sustain growth over time, and the ability of teachers and leaders to identify change initiatives as part of *the*

Table 2.2 The Cultural Proficiency Continuum: Depicting Unhealthy and Healthy Practices

Cultural Destructiveness	Cultural Incapacity	Cultural Blindness	Cultural Precompetence	Cultural Competence	Cultural Proficiency

Compliance-Based Tolerance for Diversity	Transformation for Equity
• **Cultural Destructiveness:** Seeking to eliminate references to the culture of "others" in all aspects of the school and in relationship with their communities. • **Cultural Incapacity:** Trivializing other LGBT communities and seeking to make them appear to be wrong. • **Cultural Blindness:** Pretending not to see or acknowledge the status and culture of LGBT communities and choosing to ignore the experiences of such groups within the school and community.	• **Cultural Precompetence:** Increasingly aware of what you and the school don't know about working with LGBT communities. It is at this key level of development that you and the school can move in positive, constructive direction, or you can vacillate, stop, and possibly regress. • **Cultural Competence:** Manifesting your personal values and behaviors and the school's policies and practices in a manner that is inclusive with LGBT cultures and communities that are new or different from you and the school. • **Cultural Proficiency:** Advocating for lifelong learning for the purpose of being increasingly effective in serving the educational needs of the LGBT cultural groups served by the school. Holding the vision that you and the school are instruments for creating a socially just democracy.

Source: Adapted from Terrell and Lindsey. (2009). *Culturally Proficient Leadership: The Personal Journey Begins Within.* Thousand Oaks, CA: Corwin.

Table 2.3 The Essential Elements of Cultural Proficiency

- **Assessing cultural knowledge**: Becoming aware of and knowing the LGBT communities within your school; know how educators and the school as a whole react to the LGBT communities and learn how to be effective in serving these communities. Leading and learning about the school and its grade levels and departments as cultural entities in responding to the educational needs of the LGBT communities.
- **Valuing diversity**: Creating informal and formal decision-making groups that are inclusive of parents/guardians and community members whose viewpoints and experiences are different from yours and the dominant group at the school and that will enrich conversations, decision making, and problem solving.
- **Managing the dynamics of difference**: Modeling problem solving and conflict resolution strategies as a natural and normal process within the culture of the schools and the LGBT contexts of the communities of your school.
- **Adapting to diversity**: Learning about LGBT cultural groups different from your own and the ability to use others' experiences and backgrounds in all school settings.
- **Institutionalizing cultural knowledge:** Making learning about LGBT cultural groups and their experiences and perspectives an integral part of the school's professional development.

Source: Adapted from Terrell and Lindsey. (2009). *Culturally Proficient Leadership: The Personal Journey Begins Within.* Thousand Oaks, CA: Corwin.

way we do things around here. Robert Garmston and Bruce Wellman expanded the work of Gregory Bateson and Robert Dilts by developing a model of intervention based on *the nested levels of learning* (Garmston & Wellman, 1999). Table 2.4 shows the "nested-level" model of behavioral and organizational change.

The nested-level change model (Table 2.4) displays that behavioral and observable changes most significantly occur when all levels are addressed. Change that occurs at one level impacts behaviors below that level (i.e., allocation of resources, decision making, problem solving, professional development, assessment, curriculum, and instruction decisions). Consequently, interventions that happen only at the lower levels do not impact or influence the levels above, thereby lessening the chances or opportunities for large-scale changes.

To illustrate how this model works, we need only look at school improvement efforts that begin at the two lowest levels such as providing or improving facilities, purchasing materials of instruction, and implementing new academic programs as mandated by local, state, or federal agencies. Often, educators and leaders view this method of *change* or improvement as *the answer* to the problem of the marginalization and bullying of LGBT students. Although these interventions are important and

Table 2.4 Nested Levels of Organizational Change

Identity: The individual or group's sense of self
Answers the questions: *Who are we?* or *Who am I?*

Belief system: The individual or group's values, beliefs, assumptions, and meanings
Answers the question: *Why do we do what we do?*

Capabilities: The individual and group's reflective and dialogic skills to use new knowledge, understanding, and skills
Answers the question: *How will we develop and use the skills that we have?*

Behaviors: The individual or group's actions and reactions
Answers the question: *In what specific behaviors will I or we engage?*

Environment: Basic physical surroundings, tools, materials, supplies, technology
Answers the question: *What do we need to begin?*

Source: Adapted from Lindsey, Martinez, and Lindsey. (2007). *Culturally Proficient Coaching: Supporting Educators to Create Equitable Schools.* Thousand Oaks, CA: Corwin.

necessary, they often become what we call "fill-in-the-blank" responses to problems, issues, or needs. New programs or interventions are often seen as the solution to marginalization and bullying even before student data or student needs are analyzed and appropriate questions asked. An example of this *fill-in-the-blank* reform model follows:

- *Antibullying programs* will solve the harassment problems experienced by LGBT students. Or,
- *Intervention programs* will solve the problem for those students.

Often, the *what* question is answered before the *why* question is asked. To follow this logic a bit further, we invite educators to ask this question:

- *If, _____ is the answer, what was the question?*

Was the question about student marginalization and being bullied or about student status? What data do we have, or do we need, that shows the depth of the issue? Did we select the program because of the students' needs reflected in our data? What assumptions were made about LGBT groups before data were collected? What might be other data that we need to examine?

Data-driven decisions, those decisions based on student achievement and participation data, involve educators in collaboratively selecting intervention programs, developing instructional techniques, and designing assessment strategies that reflect student needs. Westfield Unified School District educators have been engaged in collaborative conversations and data dialogues as part of their districtwide reform efforts to support LGBT students, educators, and parents/community members. The vignettes in Chapters 6 through 10 demonstrate the nested levels of commitment to large-scale change in the district.

CULTURALLY PROFICIENT LEADERSHIP LINKS BEHAVIORS WITH BELIEFS AND IDENTITY

Organizational change initiatives that focus on the lower levels of behaviors and environments fall short of impacting long-term change, whereas districts that begin change initiatives at the top of the nested-level model have a greater chance of impacting the classroom environment (i.e., lowest level) based on the influence and impact of all other levels, including the organizational identity, widely held belief systems, and skills and capabilities of organizational members (Table 2.4). Cultural Proficiency is an intervention that occurs at the upper levels of identity and belief systems. The Tools for Cultural Proficiency guide individuals and organizations to examine their values and behaviors based on their beliefs and assumptions about how students learn and who can learn. This is the *inside-out approach* for changing behaviors and environments. Once an organization's members examine who they are and for whose purpose they exist, they have a greater chance of developing skills and capabilities to address the behaviors and environments within the organization. Once programs are consistent with the organization's identity and beliefs, group members share the responsibility of developing resources in support of those agreed-upon initiatives. Westfield Unified School District is an example of members employing nested levels of organizational change.

Westfield Unified School District: A Case Story

Westfield Unified School District (WUSD) has been on a journey toward creating a culturally proficient environment so that each student in the district is working toward meeting the highest academic standards possible. Westfield is a composite narrative of many districts in Canada and the United States with whom we authors have worked as presenters and facilitators. In Chapters 6 through 10 we present narratives called "case stories." The intent of the case story is to present a true-to-life situation for you in which you are the "observer." Rather than ask you to analyze the case as in the typical case study format, we ask you to "reflect-on-action" and "reflect-for-action." We ask you to use the lens of Cultural Proficiency and reflect on what you think and what you might do as a result of your reflection.

In the case story vignettes, educators from Westfield engage in conversations that illustrate how Cultural Proficiency supports the standards-based, student-centered educational system. Table 2.5 illustrates how the Westfield Unified School District Board and superintendent along with community leaders make high expectations, rigorous curriculum, and instructional integrity explicit in policies and practices throughout the organization.

WUSD has acknowledged that the practice of Culturally Proficient LGBT programs is grounded in the district's identity as a high-performing, student-centered system. A quick review of Table 2.5 illustrates how change or clarity at the highest level of identity cascades throughout the organization. Now, take the Westfield story with you as you read Chapters 6 through 10 to enhance your skills using the Tools of Cultural Proficiency.

GOING DEEPER

Personal Reflection: Take a few minutes to think about and respond to the following questions:

- In what ways has this chapter informed and supported your learning about reflection?
- How has this chapter informed and supported your understanding about the Tools of Cultural Proficiency?
- How has your thinking about teaching and interacting with LGBT students, educators, and parents/community members been informed by reading this chapter?

_____

_____

_____

_____

Table 2.5 Nested Levels and Leverage Points for Large-Scale Change

Westfield School District Board/Trustees and Superintendent promote the district identity as high performing academically, with student-centered instruction and community engagement. The result of the district's focus is an inclusive and cohesive district goal and community-wide vision.
Answers the question: *Who are we?*

Superintendent's leadership cabinet hosts conversations/professional learning focused on districtwide mission, core values, belief statements, and public agreements. These agreements are aligned with board's goals and the district vision statement/identity.
Answers the question: *Why do we do what we do?*

District office and site leaders demonstrate high value for professional development that supports teachers and leaders by providing *Culturally Proficient Responses to Sexual Orientation in our Schools: Advocating for and Engaging with LGBT Communities* to engage teachers, counselors, administrators, and paraprofessionals in effective LGBT educational practices.
Answers the question: *How will we develop new skills and/or use the skills that we have?*

WUSD educators adopt a well-defined plan of standards-based curriculum, instruction, and assessment aligned with languages, academic needs, and cultural backgrounds of students. Educators engage in comprehensive, culturally proficient, professional learning focused on needs of LGBT students, educators, and parents/community members.
Answers the question: *In what specific behaviors will we engage?*

School site educators create supportive conditions and provide facilities, resources, and appropriate materials to engage educators in implementing standards-based curriculum, instruction, and assessment.
Answers the question: *What do we need to begin?*

Source: Adapted from Lindsey, Martinez, and Lindsey. (2007). *Culturally Proficient Coaching: Supporting Educators to Create Equitable Schools.* Thousand Oaks, CA: Corwin.

Dialogic Activity: Discuss with your colleagues and respond to the following:

- In what ways might LGBT students, educators, and parents/ community members experience barriers at your school?
- How might a student new to your school, who is heterosexual, experience your school's regard for LGBT people?
- What are your thoughts about WUSD's approach to systemwide change?
- How did the phrase "fill-in-the-blank programs" resonate with changes you have experienced as an educator?
- Please describe the mechanisms at your school to support LGBT students, educators, and parents/community members?
- What steps might you and your colleagues take to more closely examine the concepts of identity and belief systems in your environment?
- In what ways might the nested levels of commitment impact the English language and math programs in your district/school?

Chapter 3 is a critical chapter in your journey. Now that you are familiar with the Tools of Cultural Proficiency, Chapter 3 provides an opportunity for you and your colleagues to deepen and apply your knowledge, understanding, and use of two critically important concepts—equality and equity. These two terms differentiate between desired outcomes and processes used to attain those desired outcomes. As you continue your journey toward developing a school that involves LGBT members, topics, and issues, you will find Chapter 3 to be informative and useful.

3 Equality and Equity Are Both Important, Just Not the Same

We hold these truths to be self-evident, that all men are created equal, that they are endowed by their Creator with certain unalienable Rights, that among these are Life, Liberty and the pursuit of Happiness.

—U.S. Declaration of Independence, July 4, 1776 (p. 1)

GETTING CENTERED

We crafted this chapter for you to explore your views on similarities and differences of the key terms *equality* and *equity*—first as universal concepts, then, as applied to LGBT communities. We begin with a series of questions for you to consider both as an educator and as a person in this society. Think about each question and your response; you will be given an opportunity throughout the chapter to record your thinking, your reactions, and your questions. First, let's begin with your prior knowledge and experiences as an educator:

- Do you believe that in order to be fair you must treat all students, colleagues, and parents/community members *equally*?

- In what ways might you sometimes be challenged when considering *equity* as treating people differently?
- Can you treat your students, colleagues, primary caregivers, and community members who are from LGBT communities in an equitable way that compensates for the abuse and unfair treatment they have received as a group over the years? If so, what might that look like? If you responded no, describe why you responded as you do.
- Who are you in relation to people from LGBT communities? What personal insights are you learning when you think about that question?
- Have you engaged in dialogue(s) with colleagues or others about people from LGBT communities?
- What are you learning about yourself and your school from being in dialogue with colleagues?

Take a few minutes to reflect on these questions and use the space below to record your thoughts, reactions, and questions.

_____

_____

_____

_____

Your responses may be a first step in accurately describing how you position yourself in relation to LGBT issues. We invite you to stay curious and open to learning.

HISTORICAL BASES FOR EQUALITY AND EQUITY

Now that you have recorded some of your thoughts about equality and equity, let's turn your attention to the epigraph and the opening line from the U.S. Declaration of Independence. First, let's acknowledge that the context of 1776 was vastly different from present day. "All men," given the conventions of the day, excluded women. Similarly, again given the conventions of the day, it excluded slaves, free Negroes, aboriginal Americans, or most anyone who wasn't a free white male of European descent. Finally, continuing with the conventions of the day, "all men" most assuredly would not have included the LGBT communities.

So if the Declaration of Independence did not expressly include these groups, why on earth would we open with this quote as an epigraph? The answer is basic and rests on two very important historical foundations fundamental to the creation of constitutional government: (1) The U.S. Declaration of Independence has been hailed throughout the world as introducing the concept of human equality to the modern era, and (2) the Declaration of Independence paved the way for the U.S. Constitution, which laid the ground for ending slavery, extending civil rights to all (though it came in two phases—1867 and 1964),[1] and guaranteeing women's right to vote with the 1920 passage of the 19th Amendment to the U.S. Constitution. Even with all these advances, the struggle continues for equality because of inequities built into our political and economic systems and the consequent reality that many people are yet to realize equitable treatment in our democracy. The purpose of this book is to focus on one very diverse group that has been historically marginalized—the LGBT communities.

Equality and Equity: An Activity

In our work with schools over the years, confusion about equality and equity have been consistent roadblocks to addressing persistence effects of discrimination, marginalization, bias, racism, sexism, and now, heterosexism. School leaders must have operational definitions of these two important and basic concepts as we press forward to extend the basic guarantees of democracy to each and every cultural group in our schools. Our moral imperative as educators is to provide access and achievement to all cultural groups of students (Fullan, 2003).

We begin by consulting the dictionary to discern precise synonyms for equality and equity yield interesting results:

- Synonyms for *equality* include *parity, fairness, equal opportunity, impartiality*, and *egalitarianism.*
- Synonyms for *equity* include *evenhandedness, fairness, impartiality, justice, fair play*, and *justness.*

Let's begin by treating the definitions of the two terms in a purely academic exercise. What do you see as synonyms that are common to equality and equity? Please record your responses in the left column of Table 3.1, Equality and Equity: Similar and Different. Next, what do you see as differences among the synonyms? Use the right column of Table 3.1 to record your responses.

---

[1]Brief explanation that the Civil Rights Act of 1867 was never fully implemented, and the same can be argued for the Civil Rights Act of 1964. The important point to be made is provisions of the U.S. Constitution have been used to provide for equitable treatment and to press for basic civil rights in the United States.

Table 3.1 Equality and Equity: Similar and Different

Similarities	Differences

Take a few moments and think about your entries. If you are doing this exercise with colleagues, you may want to discuss your findings. When you are ready, please use the space below to record your findings along with the associated thoughts, reactions, and questions that occur to you.

_____

_____

_____

_____

From the similarities column, most likely you noticed that equality and equity have fairness and impartiality as qualities, both of which are important as human outcomes or experiences in democratic societies. Fairness and impartiality are indisputable tenets of equality as are the other alternate synonyms—parity, equal opportunity, and egalitarianism. Let's turn to the differences column. In this column, you may have noticed that equity is further defined as evenhandedness, justice, fair play, and justness. Note that equity denotes "processes" that are intended to ensure equality. Equality and equity share common characteristics of fairness and impartiality yet have important and different functions. Equity is made up of processes such as fair play and evenhandedness by intentionally treating those with less in ways intended to attain equal outcomes such as fairness and impartiality.

Equality is the goal; equity provides processes to attain that goal. Cultural Proficiency builds from a belief in equality as promised in the U.S. Declaration of Independence while recognizing that our history is one of inequity. The history of the United States since 1776 has been anything but a level playing field. This recognition of our history of inequity and the absence of level playing fields is the foundation of Cultural Proficiency's approach to equity, which embraces commitment to advocacy, social justice, and lifelong learning.

Barriers to Equality Give Way to Proactive Approaches

Systemic barriers in our society and in our schools make achieving equitable treatment and outcomes for LGBT communities an ongoing challenge. The most prevalent barriers over which we have direct influence are allowing sexual orientation and gender identity to be unmentionable topics in too many of our schools and, thereby, perpetuating a silence that stigmatizes everyone by condoning bullying and other forms of discrimination and marginalization. However, when we are proactive on values of inclusion, all students, educators/staff, and parents and community members in our school community will benefit.

Sexual Orientation and Gender Identity as Taboo Topics in Schools. Sexual orientation and gender identity continue to be deemed unmentionable topics for open discussion in schools and in our general society. The consequence of being LGBT is typically some form of bullying, physical abuse, and ostracism. These behaviors seem to be commonplace in our schools. Name-calling directed toward LGBT students is too often accompanied by whisper campaigns about the perceived sexual orientation of students, faculty, and staff. Acts of discrimination often go beyond verbal abuse and lead to people in the LGBT communities being targets of vicious physical attacks. Reports of these negative acts along with statistics on negative experiences while in schools have been compiled and reported with increased frequency.

For over a decade, the Gay Lesbian Straight Education Network (GLSEN) has been studying the experiences of LGBT students in our schools and issuing biannual reports to draw policy makers' and all educators' attention to negative experiences as well as successful efforts (Kosciw, Greytak, Bartkiewicz, Boesen, & Palmer, 2012; Kosciw, Greytak, Diaz, & Bartkiewicz, 2010). Reports of bullying, sexual harassment, and discrimination based on sexual orientation are rife in schools. Data abound that provide a graphic picture of the day-to-day reality that many LGBT persons confront. Table 3.2 contains selected data from the Executive Summary of GLSEN's 2012 report (Kosciw, Greytak, Bartkiewicz, et al., 2012). The data are vivid, but they don't tell us what to do.

To begin to resolve these dominance issues, we must acknowledge the systemic proportions of the problem, which encompass the education of all students and well-being of employees, parents, and community members. All students' education is compromised when LGBT students and faculty are objects of physical and psychological intimidation and abuse. Not only the education of targeted students is compromised, but also students, faculty, and staff who commit these acts of bullying and discrimination compromise their own moral authority as responsible citizens in a democratic society. We are now at a point in our development as a country

Table 3.2	Instances of Negative School Climate: Selected Key Findings, 2011 National Study of School Climate

LGBT Students' Experiences in Our Schools

- 71.3 % heard homophobic remarks frequently or often during the school year.
- 56.9% heard homophobic remarks from teachers or other school staff.
- 81.9% were verbally harassed because of their sexual orientation during the school year.
- 60.4% of students who were harassed or assaulted in school did not report the incident to school staff, most often believing little to no action would be taken or the situation could become worse if reported.
- 36.7% of the students who did report an incident said that school staff did nothing in response.
- 31.8% missed one entire day of school during the month of the study because of feeling unsafe or uncomfortable.

Source: Kosciw, Greytak, Bartkiewicz, et al. (2012).

and profession that we may no longer hide under the cover of silence. Time has run out for ignoring the problem. Heterosexism is now on the table; it is part of our agenda, and we must step forward to assert our individual and collective responsibilities. Our being silent carries tremendous consequences.

The Effects of Silence. Too many of us simply remain silent when hearing slurs or observing bullying. Our silence is an explicit illustration of the most pernicious point along the Cultural Proficiency Continuum. Cultural Destructiveness and the effect of our silence can promote feelings of powerlessness within us and the targets of our behavior. The resulting feelings of powerlessness by those affected limit their ability to participate fully in their own education and careers (Bochenek & Brown, 2001).

Let's make illustrations personal for a moment. If I am a member of an LGBT community and people act like they don't see me or talk about me in ways that are not who I am, then I feel like I don't exist in the context of this school or district. Being rendered invisible leads to issues of low esteem and poor academic performance for me. I'll remove myself from those who talk negatively about me. I'd rather be alone. I find that no one really understands or even wants to help. Now, I'm just lonely.

LGBT adults, too, often feel they are working in a hostile environment in much the same way that other cultural groups have been historically marginalized. LGBT persons report, "When no one talks to me or acknowledges my sexual orientation, it leaves me feeling powerless." Similarly, assuming I am a heterosexual educator who is aware of the surfacing of negative behaviors and attitudes toward LGBT communities and choose to remain silent, I, too, may experience a sense of overwhelming powerlessness. Through personal reflection and cross-cultural dialogue in faculty study groups or in professional learning sessions, possibly I can help break the silence to which I and we have silently agreed.

CHANGING THE CONTEXT

So where do you, and we, begin you might ask. When LGBT students don't see accurate portrayal of themselves in the curriculum, they can experience an invisibility that mirrors their daily existence. Over the last two generations, women, African Americans, Latinos, and other historically marginalized groups have demanded that school curricula accurately represent our social, economic, and political history. What has followed are curricula with textbooks, literature, and arts that more accurately represent society and provide authentic role models that have and continue to make major contributions to society. Literally hundreds of notable LGBT persons in all fields of endeavor represent the widest diversity of ethnic and racial groups. Yet young students who are struggling with this identity issue are not provided any models of success that they can admire. In fact the culture of the school can often become one where it seems that members of the LGBT community are despised. Hence, bullying, poor academic performance, and even increased suicide rates manifest themselves. Include curriculum that provides LGBT biographies and historical timelines, encourage straight and LGBT faculty/staff and community members to serve as role models for all students, and develop a school culture that supports the academic, physical, and psychological health of LGBT students. So begin where you are—examine curriculum, plan collaboratively for inclusive lesson and assessment strategies, and ask others to join you in seeking opportunities for change.

Concurrently, when heterosexual students are denied an authentic representation of LGBT members in our history and present society, they have a skewed vision of their own prominence reminiscent of the whitewashed curriculum of the pre–Civil Rights era. As schools deal with equity around LGBT issues, to be successful it cannot be done solely for benefit of LGBT students. Students who are not members of an LGBT community form skewed views about their peers, family members, faculty/staff members, and community members. These skewed points of view provide them and others in the society a fallacious excuse for treating LGBT members with disdain and harassment. Not knowing what one doesn't know about persons who are different from us leads to the formations of myths, beliefs in negative rumors, and ostracism. In much the same way that those who seek justice for other forms of discrimination, basic information, reflection, dialogue, and interaction have the potential of helping us to dispel myths, stereotypes, and fears. By breaking the silence, we can make progress in dealing with the marginalization and negative downward spiral as we view another targeted group.

As authors, we have observed many instances in schools and other public settings where homophobic slurs are made, sometime with malice and oftentimes through ignorant unawareness. We also observe bystanders who don't challenge the negative remarks. In these instances, silence implies consent and reinforces the offender. In some situations, students have won hard-fought battles to have gay-straight alliances certified as after-school clubs only to encounter difficulty getting a faculty sponsor. Faculty members indicated they were afraid of being stigmatized as being gay or of having their sexual orientation questioned if they stepped up to support the students' organization. Would you be willing to serve as an adviser?

Proactive Actions. Across North America, widely different protections are afforded people based on their sexual orientation and gender identity. In the province of Ontario, the home to one third of Canadians, protection from discrimination and harassment based on sexual orientation is derived from the U.N. Universal Declaration of Human Rights, asserting that *"recognition of the inherent dignity and the equal and inalienable rights of all members of the human family is the foundation of freedom, justice and peace in the world"* (U.N. Human Rights Office of the High Commissioner, 2012). In contrast within the United States, as of 2002, only the states of California, Connecticut, Vermont, and Wisconsin explicitly prohibited discrimination based on sexual orientation (Bochenek & Brown, 2001). By early 2012, twenty-two states and the District of Columbia had enacted laws prohibiting discrimination based on sexual orientation (Badgett, 2012).

In the United States, recurring efforts to expand the language of the due process clause of the 14th amendment to include protections for sexual orientation are met with stringent counterarguments within Congress and in our federal courts. California's recently signed Assembly Bill 9 is named Seth's Law for Seth Walsh, a 13-year-old who took his life in 2010 after years of harassment because of his sexual orientation and gender expression. AB 9, which is designed to protect LGBT students from discrimination, is facing fierce resistance from conservative forces trying to cast it as another example of the "gay agenda to undermine the traditional family." New York has enacted similar curricular-related legislation.

The aforementioned issues are policy and legal approaches to equity regarding sexual orientation. Additionally, we must confront personal and moral issues related to creating a safe and supportive school culture for all cultural groups, inclusive of LGBT communities. Confronting personal and moral issues is often the action of effective leaders. Breaking unofficially sanctioned silence takes bold action from leaders willing to face the moral imperative of "do the right thing." This type of leadership goes beyond holding a one-time training or information session on bullying or sexual orientation. Each of us as leaders must determine how we understand sexual orientation and gender diversity and embody that understanding into how we lead all aspects of our lives. A question to ask of ourselves is this: "Is what I am seeking to understand a technical problem, a transaction to be negotiated, or an equity issue?" All issues of diversity require leaders who know, understand, and use adaptive processes. Adaptive processes require changes in values, beliefs, and behaviors. This type of change often requires persons to experience feelings of discomfort, loss, uncertainty, and disloyalty to basic cultural and/or religious teaching. In the same vein as having conversations about race, breaking the silence, and moving toward an equitable environment for LGBT communities also requires courageous conversations. Breaking silence involves ensuring that the voices of LGBT members are present and heard. Each member must speak for himself or herself. Each reality is different.

As an educational leader, I can work to devise and implement affirmative policies, practices, and procedures in my classroom, school, district, and community. I must constantly think strategically about my professional role and be careful to do no harm as I work to support my colleagues, parents/community members, students, and school in the direction of an open, democratic community. During this same time, I must remain open and receptive to feedback while persisting with passion and purpose toward equitable outcomes.

GOING DEEPER

Personal Reflection: Take a few minutes to think about and respond to the following questions:

- What have I done, or not done, to allow bullying and other forms of discrimination against members of LGBT communities to persist in my school, organization, or community?
- In what ways do my values and espoused beliefs inform my actions to allow or interrupt discrimination against members of LGBT communities?
- How might I anticipate and address the resistance that I might encounter from colleagues, friends, and community members?

Please use the space below to record your comments, reactions, and questions.

_____

_____

_____

_____

Dialogic Activity: Reflect on your own and your colleagues' roles in providing equitable treatment to members of your school's LGBT communities.

- In what ways might you prepare, or further prepare, yourself as a Culturally Proficient leader for your school?
- What do you need to do to become part of a Culturally Proficient leadership team for your school?
- Can you be a Culturally Proficient leader if you do not address equity for members of LGBT communities? Please explain your answer.

The space below is provided for you to record your thinking and key points from your discussion.

_____

_____

_____

_____

4 Understanding Our History Helps Shape Our Future

The time is here for human rights to be inalienable.

—Raymond D. Terrell and Randall B. Lindsey (2009, p. 84)

GETTING CENTERED

Assume that you are a student, a teacher, an administrator, or a parent/guardian attending a local school function late one warm, spring afternoon. The event is a display of student work and is a well-attended annual community affair. You walk among the displays, you talk with students who are stationed near their work, and you talk with others who, like you, are keenly interested in the students' work. You are proud of your culture group, and as you walk you note that, no, your culture is hardly represented. You feel invisible. When any references are made to your cultural group, they are indirect and you are an object of other people's negative behavior. As an example, you see posters with antibullying messages and you know the intended targets are students with whom you share a cultural common ground. Antibullying messages are in some of the student displays, but you see no messages that present your culture in a positive light. Why do they always depict us as stereotypical gay people who are getting beaten up or harassed? Why can't they show the good things we have done for our communities?

Though this exercise might be hypothetical for you, try to imagine how you might react to such a scenario. Take a few moments to think about and respond to the following questions:

- In what ways might I relate to this scenario? If not, why?
- If I were an educator at this school and the person in this story confronted me, what would I say when he asked about the absence of lesbian, gay, bisexual, and transgender (LGBT) people in our curriculum and student work displays?
- Why is this story important in today's classrooms and schools?

_____

_____

_____

_____

The scenario described above could occur in any number of totalitarian countries in the 20th or 21st centuries, yet it is a common experience today for students, parents/guardians, and school educators and staff who are LGBT. Yes, antibullying messages are becoming more commonplace in our schools and, of course, we cannot assume that all bullying is focused toward LGBT communities. Furthermore, many antibullying posters/ campaigns are focused on a generalized student-to-student bullying that exists in too many of our schools. Within that context of bullying, many antibullying campaigns have emerged in response to the all-too-frequent suicides, killings, beatings, and harassment experienced by our LGBT colleagues, parents/guardians, and students. However, we must realize that as tragic as acts of bullying are, more important, they are evidence of a deeper set of issues that, when ignored and avoided, at minimum, lead to marginalization of individuals. Marginalization, in turn, leads to acts of aggression and violence. To counter these acts, antibullying programs are developed and presented as intervention programs.

Antibullying messages are substantiation that the school and the neighborhood it serves have yet

- to develop knowledge of LGBT communities,
- to display a value for being inclusive of the diverse community the school serves,
- to develop mechanisms for broaching differences, to become familiar with LGBT communities, or
- to learn about LGBT communities that reside in their midst.

Assuming you are a heterosexual person just beginning this journey in confronting your own reactions to issues of homosexuality, you might at this point, understandably, ask what the current issues outlined above have to do with our history. Likewise, if you are a member of the LGBT communities or are a LGBT ally, you might wonder aloud why others have their heads in the sand and don't see that rampant discrimination against LGBT members is not as visible in our history books as are the many fine accomplishments we prefer to showcase in our curricular materials.

NORTH AMERICAN EXCEPTIONALISM: EMERGENT CIVIL AND HUMAN RIGHTS

In this section, we provide a brief historical context of how human and civil rights issues have been a constant and consistent historical struggle with particular emphasis on the United States and Canada. Our intent is to illustrate the presence of LGBT people in the history and culture of the United States and Canada. We are not presenting an exhaustive treatise on prominent historical figures, merely making the case that our society has always been diverse in terms of sexual orientation. Our history books often promote the United States as being a "nation of immigrants" as one of our mighty strengths and benefits of diversity. Notwithstanding the immigrant image of America, not everyone who came to these shores did so willingly and we must also acknowledge that a vibrant multilingual, multicultural society was in place well before the arrival of European explorers. One of the rarely discussed historical consequences of our diversity has been discrimination.

Much talk abounds in the United States these days about American exceptionalism. In fact, the term *American exceptionalism* has become a litmus test in some political quarters for determining one's level of patriotism. We, the authors, make it clear that U.S. democracy has spawned great accomplishments in political, economic, and social realms that continue to reverberate around the world. We propose a facet to American exceptionalism that is rarely discussed and is what makes our democracy unique—namely, that the framers of the U.S. Constitution provided means by which the social contract envisioned by Jefferson and colleagues could be expanded and amended. As the society matured from a loose confederation of states to a centralized federal government, it slowly ensured the gradual expansion of civil and human rights. In our over 200 years of history, this country remedied or put to an end, often with great resistance, legalized discrimination.

Sanctioned discrimination is an ugly, and unavoidable, part of the history of the United States and Canada. We, the authors, intentionally use the word *unavoidable,* because to end discrimination and marginalization begins with being brave enough to learn about these societal ills that have been fostered and allowed to flourish in our countries. We also know, in the United States and Canada, that many people prefer to avoid learning about our histories of legal-based discrimination that moved indigenous people to reserves, that remanded citizens of Japanese ancestry to relocation centers, or that sought to limit women to second-class status. Similarly, we know from the recent history of the Civil Rights Movement in the United States that racism as a set of economic, political, and social issues had to be addressed if the United States was to progress and if racism was to be countered. The continued struggle of African Americans and Native First Nations people and their allies to rectify the legacy of racism provides a perspective that American exceptionalism is not a fully realized dream. The continuous efforts toward social, political, and economic equity by African Americans and Native First Nations people provides a perspective for an American exceptionalism that confronts forms of systemic discrimination. With this book, we make a particular emphasis on confronting and overcoming heterosexism.

To provide a point of view for sanctioned discrimination against LGBT communities, you may find it helpful to review examples of legalized discrimination with which you may be more familiar—namely, discrimination based on race, ethnicity, and gender. African Americans were regarded as property in the United States during the formal period of slavery from 1619 to 1863 and were denied basic civil rights during the Jim Crow era of 1863 to 1954. Since the Civil War, African Americans have had to use every legal process in the three branches of government to be amended into the social contract in order to participate in the educational, political, and economic fortunes of this country. One of our (authors') heroes from the modern U.S. civil rights movement of the 1950s and 1960s is Dr. Terrence Roberts, a well-known historical personage as one of the Little Rock Nine high school students who integrated Central High School in 1957. We had the opportunity to participate in one of Dr. Roberts's seminars at the Museum of Tolerance[1] where he provided a perspective on our 335 years of legalized discrimination. Table 4.1 chronicles the types of discrimination and legal consequences of discrimination that are part of a history that many would like to ignore or, maybe even worse, to minimize as inconsequential to today's realities.

After pointing out our history of 335 years of putting practices into place that legalized discrimination, Dr. Roberts then notes that we are now into our sixth decade of dismantling those highly institutionalized practices. He would say, "335 years to create the situation on the one

---

[1]Los Angeles, California, January 31, 2012.

Table 4.1   Sanctioned Racial Discrimination and Countermeasures

1619—1863+	=	244 years	Slavery legal in United States
1863—1954+	=	91 years	Jim Crow; Restrictive covenants
1954—2001	=	47 years	*Brown v. Topeka Board of Education*
2002—2012	=	10 years	NCLB and state initiatives

hand and 60 years to rectify the situation." Is there any wonder why we have an achievement gap in the United States? Maybe even more important, the achievement gap has been nationally acknowledged only with the advent of No Child Left Behind in 2002—a scant ten years as of this writing!

Across North America, racial and ethnic discrimination is also a historical and current experience of the aboriginal communities of First Nations, Inuit, and Métis.[2] Aboriginal communities have a history of treaties with Canadian and U.S. governments that provided "country within country" status, only to have those promises repeatedly violated when in the best interests of the dominant society. In both countries, litigation and recompense negotiations have been underway for generations; all the while, unemployment, underemployment, and educational disparities have been allowed to persist.

Yet the modern histories of our two countries diverge when it comes to LGBT communities. Though the recording of history has rendered LGBT people somewhat invisible to the dominant culture, such invisibility must not be allowed to minimize the reality that the human population has always experienced a rich diversity of sexual orientations. To gain a perspective on how history and literature have been recorded, one has only to turn the calendar back a few years ago and recall the extent to which women and people of color were invisible in the history and literature books used in our schools. Students of today would find it rather odd if their books did not reflect the prominent historical and current roles of women and people of color throughout all sectors of society. The extent to which people do or do not appear in the recorded history or literature of our textbooks is a function of who compiled the books and who publishes and markets the books, not of people's actual roles and contributions to any society or culture.

---

[2]Métis refers to aboriginal people in Canada who trace ancestry to First Nations and French heritage.

What may be new is that more people will now know what only a small part of society has known all along—that our history and culture is replete with the presence of LGBT people. So, you might ask, how did this invisibility occur? Good question. In Chapter 2, you learned that the Cultural Proficiency approach is an *inside-out* process, so once again, let's begin with what you do know.

ACTIVITY

Think about your knowledge of prominent people from the history of your country. Name two or three LGBT people who made contributions to literature, sciences, business, the arts, or history prior to 1930. Use the space below to record your thinking. Now, name two or three LGBT people who are now contributing to literature, sciences, business, the arts, or history. Try to avoid listing current celebrity entertainers. Again, use the space below to list your responses.

_____

_____

_____

_____

Reflections

Take a few minutes to think about and respond to the following questions:

- What is your reaction to this activity?
- To what extent were you successful in naming people?
- If you were able to list prominent people, how did you know them?
- If you were unable to list only a few or none at all, speculate on why you were at a disadvantage with this activity?
- Please use the space below to record your thoughts, reactions, and feelings.

_____

_____

_____

_____

Heteronormative Worldviews. If you, like many of us, struggled with this basic activity, you may hold a heteronormative worldview. Relax, this is not an indictment; rather, it is naming our experience so we can be mindful and intentional in our learning. A heteronormative worldview is holding a view, or system of belief, based in the assumption that everyone is heterosexual (Corbin, 2011, p. 2). A heteronormative worldview is distinctly different from homophobia, which is an unexamined fear of homosexuals. You have the power to broaden your worldview, which, we posit, may assist in examining unexamined fears and biases.

Our country's evolving awareness of educational issues of race, ethnicity, national origin, language, gender, social class, faith, age, and ableness is expanding in ways that provide members of these demographic groups opportunities in our school that would have been unheard of a generation or two ago. However, the same does not extend to students who are homosexual, perceived to be homosexual, or who hide their identity to gain acceptance from others. Corbin (2011), in her study of homosexual students' experiences with heterosexism, found that the consequence is an internal suffering that leads to students' invalidating their authentic selves (p. 110).

Educators need to know and understand that gender diversity and sexual orientation have always been with us. Gender diversity and sexual orientation are not new to the human experience. What may be new is that we are beginning to recognize the woeful limits of our actions and becoming resolved in responding to the educational and social needs of the students, faculty/staff, and parents/guardians from our LGBT communities.

HISTORICAL PERSPECTIVE

Same-sex relations have been evident throughout the history of humankind (Campos, 2005; Sullivan, 2008). Whether ancient Rome or Athens, medieval Japan or China, pre-European Africa, or the many tribes of North America, social roles for men and women found same-sex relations acceptable. In fact, evidence suggests that the distinctions made in the United States and Canada about same-sex relations was varied among previous cultures. For instance, Native American Indian tribes did not distinguish among people through the use of terms such as *gay, lesbian,* or *transgender.* Miller (2006) notes that "the homosexual of the ancient world was Everyman, not a specific 'type'" (p. xvi).

Prior to the arrival of Europeans to North America, the aboriginal communities across the continent acknowledged homosexual relationships. Ethnohistorian Walter Williams found *berdaches,* men who often wore women's clothing and performed women's roles and performed sacred roles in tribal rituals, evident in 130 North American tribes. Williams noted that berdaches were looked down on by more warlike tribes such as the

Comanche and Apache but were revered by the Navajo tribes. In communities where they were respected, *two-spirit people* replaced the term berdache. The term berdache fell into disfavor with the arrival of white explorers, settlers, and missionaries. The arrival of white men introduced a negative judgment on the term berdache, which assigned a derogatory Persian definition of a passive homosexual partner, a connotation not found in the North American tribes (Miller 2006, pp. 30–31).

Meanwhile in medieval Europe, evidence of oppression is well recognized into the 19th and 20th centuries. In 1869, the first documented use of the term *homosexuality* was in an anonymous pamphlet in Germany calling for repeal of sodomy laws (Miller, 2006, p. xi). In 20th-century Nazi Germany, homosexuals were considered incarnations of moral degeneracy in the same way they regarded Jews and others deemed to threaten the perceived purity of the German "race" (Miller, 2006, p. 195).

As the 20th century dawned in North America, LGBT communities were both oppressed and emerging. Sodomy laws, discrimination of all types, and rendering homosexuals invisible were well-institutionalized practices across the continent. In seeming contrast, LGBT communities proliferated in urban centers of the United States and Canada, most notably in literary circles. A dichotomy of silent recognition of LGBT literary contributions, often by members using pseudonyms without acknowledgment of sexual orientation or gender identity, in the larger community were accompanied by unspeakable acts of bullying and irrational fears of homophobia. The combination of repression and fear led to suppressive systems throughout society. Late in the 20th century, LGBT communities coalesced to push back against institutional forms of oppression and repression. Resistance to personal and institutional repression was made manifest when the term *heterosexism* was used to name the oppression felt by LGBT people and communities for no reason other than their sexual orientation.

HETEROSEXISM AND HUMAN RIGHTS

As we were preparing the final draft of this manuscript, the U.N. Human Rights Office of the High Commissioner (2012) issued a seminal report that opens with this perspective:

> The case for extending the same rights to lesbian, gay, bisexual and transgender (LGBT) persons as those enjoyed by everyone else is neither radical nor complicated. It rests on two fundamental principles that underpin international human rights law: equality and non-discrimination. The opening words of the Universal Declaration of Human Rights are unequivocal: "All human beings are born free and equal in dignity and rights."

The report concludes, in part, that

> protecting LGBT people from violence and discrimination does not require the creation of a new set of LGBT specific rights, nor does it require the establishment of new international human rights standards. For all the heat and complexity of the political debate about LGBT Equality at the United Nations, from a legal perspective the issue is straightforward. The obligations that States (i.e., countries) have to protect LGBT persons from violations of their human rights are already well established and are binding on all United Nations Member States. (p. 7)

Our intent in this section is to demonstrate that the legal and moral bases for respecting LGBT communities exist both within international communities and the sovereign nations of the United States and Canada. However, compliance with such mandates is often not sufficient and leads to minimum efforts. The work of Cultural Proficiency involves educators' embracing the work of diversity and equity as moral frames for doing what is right in society. We endeavored to provide this brief review to describe the evolutionary nature of human and civil rights. The time is now to continue the journey in ways that create validation for LGBT communities as full members of society and, thereby, a similar validation for heterosexual communities to replace personal and systemic discrimination with inclusive personal behaviors and systemic practices.

THE TOOLS OF CULTURAL PROFICIENCY FRAME CHALLENGES AND OPPORTUNITIES

Now that you have this brief history review, what can you do to move forward? We recommend using the Tools of Cultural Proficiency to guide your journey toward creating an equitable, supportive educational environment for LGBT students. In Chapter 2, the Tools of Cultural Proficiency were presented and described as means for individuals and schools to take responsibility for learning how to be effective in working with LGBT communities, both the communities within the school and the communities served by the school. The Tools can be understood as a 3-pronged process:

• *Framing challenges and opportunities.* The Cultural Proficiency Continuum is to be used to display, understand, and communicate challenges and opportunities. Behaviors and actions that appear to the left side of the Continuum—Cultural Destructiveness, Cultural Incapacity, and Cultural Blindness—are the challenges and obstructions that result in discrimination and marginalization. Conversely, behaviors and actions that occur on the right side of the Continuum—Cultural Precompetence, Cultural Competence, and Cultural Proficiency—are the opportunities we have created that ensure that LGBT communities are fully included in the academic and social life of the school.

- *Developing an ethical framework.* The Guiding Principles are deeply held core values that (a) acknowledge the existence of heterosexist practices that lead to heteronormative worldviews and (b) lead people and organizations to develop values and policies that frame individual behaviors and schoolwide practices.

- *Doing the work.* The Five Essential Elements build on the Guiding Principles of Cultural Proficiency and guide personal actions and organizational practices.

GOING DEEPER

Personal Reflection: Take a few minutes to think about and respond to the following questions:

- What have you learned in this chapter?
- What prior learning was supported?
- What prior learning was challenged?
- What questions do you have at this time?

Please use the space below to record your responses.

_____

_____

_____

_____

Dialogic Activity: Take a few minutes to think about and discuss with colleagues the following:

- In what ways might your school invalidate LGBT students' views of themselves?
- In what ways might your school contribute to other students' restricted views of LGBT students?

- In what ways does your school authentically involve LGBT educators and staff?
- In what ways does your school authentically involve LGBT parents/guardians?

As you engage colleagues in dialogue, use the space below to record your thinking and your questions. Don't be afraid to be curious.

_____

_____

_____

_____

SUGGESTED FURTHER READING

For this chapter we are including the following recommendations for further reading. Each reference can be used for book studies, either alone or with colleagues.

Campos, David. (2005). *Understanding gay and lesbian youth: Lessons for straight school teachers, counselors, and administrators.* Lanham, MD: Rowman & Littlefield Education.

DeWitt, Peter. (2012). *Dignity for all: Safeguarding LGBT students.* Thousand Oaks, CA: Corwin.

Miller, Neil. (2006). *Out of the past: Gay and lesbian history from 1869 to the present.* New York: Alyson Books.

Sullivan, Michael K. (2008). Homophobia, history, and homosexuality: Trends for sexual minorities. *Journal of Human Behavior in the Social Environment, 8*(2/3), 247–260. doi:10.1300/J137v08n02_01

Part II

Westfield Unified School District

EQUITY AND INCLUSION OF LGBT COMMUNITIES

You are invited, challenged, and supported throughout this book to learn and apply the Essential Elements of Cultural Proficiency to your behaviors and your school's practices in ways that result in lesbian, gay, bisexual, and transgender (LGBT) members being full-fledged participants in your school and district. Chapter 5 provides parameters for developing school as a safe space for all students, their families, and school employees. Chapters 6 through 10 each builds on the concept of safe space by describing each Essential Element as a standard for educator behavior and school policy development inclusive of LGBT colleagues, students, and parents/ community members. We present the Essential Elements in separate chapters to facilitate deep study and mastery of each of the Elements. However, in practice the Elements are interdependent and with practice are manifestations of your core values that support equity and diversity. Table II.1 provides descriptions of the five Essential Elements of Cultural Competence. Chapters 6 through 10 each opens with the definition of the Essential Element covered in that chapter, specifically applied for support with LGBT communities.

Westfield Unified School District

In Chapters 6 through 10, you will meet teachers, students, administrators, counselors, and parents/community members from Westfield

Table II.1   Culturally Proficient Approaches With LGBT Communities: Using the Essential Elements of Cultural Competence

Assess Culture: Listen to yourself to accurately assess what you know about yourself in relation to LGBT communities. Next, listen to your colleagues to hear their personal stories, concerns, and attitudes about sexual orientation and gender identity. The ability to assess your own, your colleagues', and your school's cultural knowledge provides important information about the extent to which you facilitate or impede inclusivity.

Value Diversity: Model inclusive language and practices as a way to let people know that your organization is a safe environment. Use terms that reflect your knowledge of and comfort with LGBT and straight communities.

Manage the Dynamics of Difference: Proactively address all levels of conflict as natural and normal events, including micro-aggressions and micro-assaults. State clearly that when personal beliefs clash with the organization's commitment to diversity and equity, the organization's core values are paramount.

Adapt to Diversity: Provide professional development for educators that meets the academic and social needs of LGBT students, faculty/staff, and community members. Develop a culture of holding one another responsible for appropriate language and behavior. Assist colleagues as they adjust to new ideas and ways of supporting LGBT communities.

Institutionalize Cultural Knowledge: Engage yourself and lead colleagues in examining personal beliefs and organizational values that support justice for and equity with LGBT communities. Engage colleagues in conversations to deepen understandings and attitudes of being a diverse and inclusive learning community. Review professional development curricula to ensure inclusivity of topics and issues that affect LGBT colleagues, students, and community members.

Unified School District. The case stories in the chapters are represented as composite experiences with members of schools, districts, and other organizations with whom we have worked. From study of the chapters, you will learn the manner in which the Essential Element covered in a particular chapter relates to you as well as to your colleagues, students, and parents/community members. At points throughout the chapters, you are provided the opportunity to reflect on your reading and on your professional experiences. The final section of each chapter presents a Going Deeper section posing two opportunities for your consideration:

- A personal reflection activity for you to think more deeply about your role as an educator and the commitments you are willing to make to extend your own learning about LGBT issues and topics

- A dialogic activity for you and your colleagues to consider your community's commitment to continuous professional learning about LGBT issues and topics

As you will read in Chapter 6, the Board of Education of Westfield Unified School District has had a goal for the past three years to focus on closing the education gap for learners who need to be served differently. Concomitantly, along with the board's Priority One! Close the Gap initiative, the superintendent and his leadership team launched a plan to study the district's culture and climate for managing equity and inclusion of LGBT communities. The board, superintendent, and leadership team as well as parents and community members want to create a safe, caring environment for all students and employees in the district. The case stories in Chapters 6 through 10 provide a glimpse of culturally proficient educational practices in action. WUSD district administrators, principals, counselors, teachers, and parents work together to move forward the change initiative in ways that value all learners and lead to better and safer school experiences.

The Essential Elements are integrated and made interdependent in Chapter 11, Part III, in a cohesive manner for the individual reader and groups of educators to develop ways to enrich the school culture through meaningful inclusion of your LGBT colleagues, students, and parents/ community members. Chapter 11 guides you to be reflective and proactive in using the language and Tools of Cultural Proficiency for yourself and with your colleagues.

5 Creating Safe Space: Moving From Compliance to Advocacy

It is OK to have your belief system, but it is not OK to use it to oppress others.

—Richard Diaz (personal communication, June 29, 2011)

GETTING CENTERED

Data that describe incidences of bullying in our schools are well known and readily available. We are witnesses almost every day to reports about bullying in its various forms. Sometimes bullying is described as cyberattacks on children and youth focused on "who is liked and who is not liked." Often, bullying is in terms of racial, gender, religious, ethnic, social class, or ableness bias. Wherever the source and whoever is impacted, bullying in our schools is not new and has been the bane of administrators, school board members, teachers, students, and parents/guardians for generations. Irrespective of what has been with us in the past, two new issues have emerged in recent years that have propelled bullying to the national stage. One new issue is that because of the proliferation of types of social media, the general public is more aware of bullying than at any other time in our history. The second "new" issue is bullying that focuses on gender identity and sexual orientation is no longer a well-kept secret and has, finally, been made a front-and-center topic in our schools.

Think about your school for a few moments because we intend to prompt your curiosity.

- What is your school's formal policy regarding bullying?
- To what extent is the policy enforced?
- How many acts of bullying toward students, faculty/staff, or parents were reported last school year?
- Describe your school's antibullying program.
- To what extent does your school's antibullying program address issues of gender identity and sexual orientation?
- Why or why not should your school have an antibullying program?
- As you read these questions, what questions arise in your thinking about bullying and your school's role in creating safe spaces for all students and adults?

Please use the space below to record your responses to these prompts and to record questions that arise in your thinking.

_____

_____

_____

_____

WHAT IS BULLYING?

A prior, broadly accepted definition of bullying indicates that victims are exposed to negative actions by one person or groups of people repeatedly over time (Olweus, 1993). Today, we suggest that definition holds true and is even more substantiated by negative acts of cyberharassment, gay bashing, and parent-led acts of revenge on peers of their children. Perhaps the real tragedy involving bullying is the reluctance of victims to report these repeated actions against them. WestEd researchers studied and reported (Petrosino, Guckenburg, DeVoe, & Hanson, 2010) the Department of Justice's 2007 National Crime Victimization Survey School Crime Supplement to determine the bullying incidents of children who attended school in the prior academic year. The report indicated students were considered bullied if they responded affirmatively to having been bullied in one or more of the following ways:

- Being made fun of
- Being the subject of rumors

- Being threatened with harm
- Being pushed, shoved, tripped, or spit on
- Being made to do things they did not want to do
- Being intentionally excluded from activities
- Having property intentionally destroyed (p. 17)

The report also indicated that the difficulty with addressing bullying in schools is that many target students and groups of students do not report acts of bullying. Many bullying incidents occur outside the school day, and school officials are not aware of the details surrounding the incidents. And compounding the problems for target students is that some parents, educators, and school officials continue to see these incidents as "kids being kids" and do not see a victim at all. Therefore, the victim is even more marginalized and left alone and lonely.

The data on bullying are alarming, but not new. Maybe it is true that with the advent of many forms of mass communications and social media, bullying is better reported than in the past. Furthermore, cyberbullying has created a new awareness of the detachment afforded bullies. Since bullying is ultimately an expression of power, the relative invisibility of cyberspace appears to embolden many to be even more ruthless in their bullying.

You, the reader, don't necessarily need data to convince you that bullying is an issue; antibullying may be one compelling reason you are reading this book. You don't need to be convinced that bullying exists; you are seeking support and resources to help eliminate bullying. In this chapter, we review data on bullying to provide a context for describing the manner in which the Tools of Cultural Proficiency can effectively support you and your school in confronting bullying in a manner that is both systemic for the school and individually for you the educator. Defining the problem helps develop a mind-set for addressing the problem.

WHY DO PEOPLE BULLY?

The question of why people bully is of paramount importance for educators dedicated to devising approaches to lessen and eliminate bullying in our schools. The U.S. Department of Health and Human Services website, stopbullying.gov, poses several reasons as to why people bully:

- Cultural causes: When the culture is "fascinated with winning, power, and violence," leading to some people believing violence is an appropriate way to gain power
- Institutional causes: When home or school does not have high standards for the way people treat one another

- Social issues: When acting out gets more attention than acting courteously or civilly and is coupled with lack of personal and social skills
- Family issues: When children and youth are from families that are not warm and loving or are from families with inconsistent monitoring and constructive discipline methods
- Bully's personal history: When children and youth experience social rejection themselves and/or experience academic failure
- Having power: When people have power without the leadership skills for wielding power effectively (U.S. Department of Health and Human Services, 2012b)

Take a moment and return to Table 2.2, the Cultural Proficiency Continuum, to note that the causes of bullying summarized above are all located on the left side of the continuum. On the left side of the continuum, cultures are oppressed and marginalized. Please keep the continuum in mind as you read this chapter and review current data on bullying and as you are introduced to our two-phase approach to bullying. One very significant thing to keep in mind as you proceed with this chapter is being able to "see" bullying. You have to recognize and acknowledge bullying before devising and implementing an effective approach to mitigating and eliminating bullying as it affects your students, your faculty/staff colleagues, and members of your community.

CURRENT DATA ON BULLYING

In an important report (Robers, Zhang, & Truman, 2010), the National Center for Education Statistics' School Survey on Crime and Safety canvassed school principals about disciplinary problems in their schools. The researchers examined disciplinary problems as daily or weekly occurrences of student racial/ethnic tensions, bullying, sexual harassment of other students, verbal abuse of teachers, acts of disrespect for teachers other than verbal abuse, and widespread disorder in the classroom. Within the larger context of disciplinary problems, principals reported 25% instances of disciplinary problems across grade levels being bullying. When broken down by grade levels, 44% of bullying as disciplinary reports were at the middle school level, with 22% and 21% at the high school and elementary school levels, respectively (p. 30).

Within the context of school experiences, the Gay, Lesbian and Straight Education Network (GLSEN) sought to learn the experiences of lesbian, gay, bisexual, and transgender youth in U.S. schools. Their powerful, authoritative national school climate survey gauged these negative indicators of school climate:

- Hearing biased remarks, including homophobic remarks, in school
- Feeling unsafe in school because of personal characteristics, such as sexual orientation, gender expression, or race/ethnicity
- Missing classes or days of school because of safety reasons
- Experiences of harassment and assault in school (Kosciw, Greytak, Bartkiewicz, Boesen, & Palmer, 2012)

Bullying as experienced by lesbian, gay, bisexual, and transgender children and youth leads to a hostile school climate and high rates of absenteeism. We invite you, an experienced adult, and most likely an educator, to slowly review the data in Table 5.1 and think about your school context as you respond to the following question. To what extent are homophobic remarks, verbal abuse, and physical harassment and abuse like these occurring in your school?

Table 5.1 Reported Instances of Hostile Climate: 2011 National School Climate Survey

- 84.9% of students heard *gay* used in a negative way (e.g., "that's so gay") frequently or often at school, and 86.5% reported that they felt distressed to some degree by this.
- 71.3% heard other homophobic remarks (e.g., *dyke* or *faggot*) frequently or often at school.
- 61.4% heard negative remarks about gender expression (not acting "masculine enough" or "feminine enough") frequently or often at school.
- 63.5% felt unsafe at school because of their sexual orientation, and 39.9%, because of how they expressed their gender.
- 81.9% were verbally harassed (e.g., called names or threatened) at school because of their sexual orientation, and 63.7%, because of their gender expression.
- 38.3% were physically harassed (e.g., pushed or shoved) at school in the past year because of their sexual orientation, and 27.2%, because of their gender expression.
- 18.3% were physically assaulted (e.g., punched, kicked, injured with a weapon) because of their sexual orientation, and 12.5%, because of their gender expression.
- 55.2% of LGBT students were harassed or threatened by their peers via electronic mediums (e.g., text messages, e-mails, instant messages, or postings on Internet sites such as Facebook), often known as cyberbullying.
- 60.4% of students who were harassed or assaulted in school did not report the incident to school staff, believing little or no action would be taken or the situation could become worse if reported.
- 36.7% of the students who did report an incident said that school staff did nothing in response.

Source: Kosciw, Greytak, Bartkiewicz, Boesen, and Palmer. (2012).

The GLSEN report noted that school staff members rarely intervened on behalf of lesbian, gay, bisexual, and transgender (LGBT) students. Stop for a moment and think about that observation—school staff members rarely intervened on behalf of LGBT students! The impact of these egregious acts of bullying and harassment is denial of an equitable access to education described in Chapter 3. With little support from adults at the school, the manner in which many LGBT students cope is to miss school so as not to face relentless harassment. Note the following data:

- 29.8% of students skipped a class at least once in the past month because they felt unsafe or uncomfortable.
- 31.8% missed at least one entire day of school in the past month because they felt unsafe or uncomfortable.
- Students were three times as likely to have missed classes (57.9% vs. 19.6%) and twice as likely to have missed at least one day of school (53.2% vs. 20.4%) in the past month because they felt unsafe or uncomfortable, when compared to the general population of secondary school students (Kosciw, Greytak, Bartkiewicz, et al., 2012).

Reflection

Take a few moments to review the data in the section above. What thoughts are occurring for you? What are your reactions to the data? What questions are surfacing for you? What new questions about your school or district might be surfacing for you? Please use the space below to record your responses.

_____

_____

_____

_____

TWO-PHASE RESPONSE TO BULLYING

Bullying has created a growing industry of programmatic responses to bullying. Our intent is

- to suggest guidelines for compliance to legal and ethical standards, and
- to use the Tools of Cultural Proficiency to move beyond compliance to embracing a moral framework for enduring professional practice and institutional policies.

Where and how you begin this process, is not as important as why you begin to take constructive action. You will take action to make discernible progress and to positively affect the lives of students, teachers/staff, and members of the community. For ease of explanation and description we use a two-phase approach that is overlapped and intertwined.

- Phase I: Key components for antibullying laws and policies described by the U.S. Department of Health and Human Services.
- Phase II: The Essential Elements of Cultural Competence as standards for professional values and behavior as well as for school policies and practices.

Phase I: Components for Antibullying Policies

The U.S. Department of Health and Human Services website stopbullying.gov has indispensable information for use by you and your school as you craft antibullying programs. Components identified from state laws that may be most useful for your planning are summarized below. When you access the website stopbullying.gov, each of the components listed below is accompanied by a link that provides examples for the component.

Table 5.2 Components to Consider in Planning Antibullying Programs

Purpose statement

- Outlines the range of detrimental effects bullying has on students, including impacts on student learning, school safety, student engagement, and the school environment.
- Declares that any form, type, or level of bullying is unacceptable, and that every incident needs to be taken seriously by school administrators, school staff (including teachers), students, and students' families.

Statement of scope—Covers conduct that occurs on the school campus, at school-sponsored activities or events (regardless of the location), on school-provided transportation, or through school-owned technology or that otherwise creates a significant disruption to the school environment.

Specification of prohibited conduct

- Provides a specific definition of bullying that includes a clear definition of cyberbullying. The definition of bullying includes a nonexclusive list of specific behaviors that constitute bullying and specifies that bullying includes intentional efforts to harm one or more individuals, may be direct or indirect, is not limited to behaviors that cause physical harm, and may be verbal (including oral and written language) or nonverbal. The definition of bullying can be easily understood and interpreted by school boards, policy makers, school administrators, school staff, students, students' families, and the community.

- Is consistent with other federal, state, and local laws.
- Prohibited conduct also includes the following:
  o Retaliation for asserting or alleging an act of bullying
  o Perpetuating bullying or harassing conduct by spreading hurtful or demeaning material even if the material was created by another person (e.g., forwarding offensive e-mails or text messages)

Enumeration of specific characteristics

- Explains that bullying may include, but is not limited to, acts based on actual or perceived characteristics of students who have historically been targets of bullying and provides examples of such characteristics.
- Makes clear that bullying does not have to be based on any particular characteristic.

Development and implementation of local education agency (LEA) policies— Directs every LEA to develop and implement a policy prohibiting bullying, through a collaborative process with all interested stakeholders, including school administrators, staff, students, students' families, and the community, in order to best address local conditions.

Components of LEA policies

- **Definitions:** Includes a definition of bullying consistent with the definitions specified in state law.
- **Report bullying:** Includes a procedure for students, students' families, staff, and others to report incidents of bullying, including a process to submit such information anonymously and with protection from retaliation. The procedure identifies and provides contact information for the appropriate school personnel responsible for receiving the report and investigating the incident.

  Requires that school personnel report, in a timely and responsive manner, incidents of bullying they witness or are aware of to a designated official.
- **Investigating and responding to bullying:** Includes a procedure for promptly investigating and responding to any report of an incident of bullying, including immediate intervention strategies for protecting the victim from additional bullying or retaliation, and includes notification to parents of the victim, or reported victim, of bullying and the parents of the alleged perpetrator and, if appropriate, notification to law enforcement officials.
- **Written records:** Includes a procedure for maintaining written records of all incidents of bullying and their resolution.
- **Sanctions:** Includes a detailed description of a graduated range of consequences and sanctions for bullying.

(Continued)

Table 5.2 (Continued)

- **Referrals:** Includes a procedure for referring the victim, perpetrator, and others to counseling and mental and other health services, as appropriate.

  Communication plan—Includes a plan for notifying students, students' families, and staff of policies related to bullying, including the consequences for engaging in bullying.

Training and preventive education

- Includes a provision for school districts to provide training for all school staff, including, but not limited to, teachers, aides, support staff, and school bus drivers, on preventing, identifying, and responding to bullying.
- Encourages school districts to implement age-appropriate school- and community-wide bullying prevention programs.

Transparency and monitoring

- Includes a provision for LEAs to report annually to the state on the number of reported bullying incidents and any responsive actions taken.
- Includes a provision for LEAs to make data regarding bullying incidence publicly available in aggregate with appropriate privacy protections to ensure students are protected.

  Statement of rights to other legal recourse—Includes a statement that the policy does not preclude victims from seeking other legal remedies.

Source: U.S. Department of Health and Human Services. (2012a)

Reflection

- What components does your school's antibullying program include?
- How effective is the program on discouraging bullying at your school?
- In what ways might the antibullying program be assessed for effectiveness?
- What might be additional resources for your school to address the needs of students who are being bullied?

Use the space below for your responses or new questions that occur to you.

_____

_____

_____

_____

Programs to Respond to Bullying

The following are organizations that offer programs designed to confront, reduce, and eliminate bullying in our schools. The organizations represented here are from our personal knowledge and, by no means, are an exhaustive list. Take a moment to access their websites to view the programs and services they offer.

- GLSEN: The Gay, Lesbian and Straight Education Network's website has a cornucopia of materials that are authoritative, free, and downloadable (glsen.org).
- Jer's Vision: Works to eliminate bullying, homophobia, transphobia, and other forms of discrimination in schools and youth communities across Canada and the United States. Their website offers programs and downloadable materials (jersvision.org).
- Hazelden Foundation: Offers the Olewus Bullying Prevention Program of materials, training, and resources (violencepreventionworks.org).
- Southern Poverty Law Center: Provides free publications such as *Teaching Tolerance* and the standards-aligned kit *Bullied: A Student, a Case, and School That Made History* (splcenter.org).
- Resource D at the back of this book offers many additional resources for educator and community member use that we culled from our review of online sources.

Phase II: Beyond Compliance: Standards for Professional and School Practice

You may want to review Chapter 2 again and refresh your recollection of the Tools of Cultural Proficiency. One tool, the Cultural Proficiency Continuum, frames unhealthy and healthy responses to bullying. Another tool, the Essential Elements, includes the standards that frame healthy values and behaviors for individuals and, at the same time, serve as a frame or guide for school policies and practices. The inside-out feature of Cultural Proficiency, described in Chapter 2, is an initial step in developing a mind-set for personal transformation and educational reform. Cross (1989) and Campos (2005), in their seminal works, locate institutional reform as beginning with the recognition that for systemic change to occur it must begin with a consideration of how professionals view themselves in relation to the populations they serve. In the case of this book, our focus is on educators' relationship to the LGBT populations in schools and communities.

Culturally Proficient learning and leadership are distinguished from other diversity and equity approaches in that Cultural Proficiency is anchored in the belief that people must clearly understand their own assumptions, beliefs, and values about people and cultures different from themselves in order to be effective in cross-cultural settings. Chapters 6 through 10 guide you through a step-by-step process in examining assumptions, beliefs, policies, and practices in a manner that leads to the development of culturally inclusive schools.

Basic to developing a Culturally Proficient approach for you and your school is developing an understanding of the following:

- The extent of the problem of bullying in general
- Bullying as visited on LGBT communities
- Resources available to you
- The importance of being proactive in bullying prevention

The five Essential Elements are proactive behavior grounded in moral values of the Guiding Principles. Chapters 6 through 10 are each devoted to one Essential Element, and each chapter is designed for you to learn the element and to decide the manner in which you will use the element to guide your work and that of your school in providing for the educational needs of LGBT students.

Interwoven through Chapters 6 through 10 are case story vignettes that present, describe, discuss, and provide multiple perspectives to integrate into practice proactive stances for the prevention of bullying:

- Parent/guardian perspectives
- Student perspectives
- Educator perspectives (teacher, counselor, teacher aide, youth worker)
- Principal/administrator perspectives
- Board of Education perspectives
- Community perspectives

GOING DEEPER

Personal Reflection: By staying with us to this point in the book, you have demonstrated your commitment to your own learning. Maybe even more important, you are demonstrating a commitment to learning for the benefit of the students and community you serve.

- In what ways has this chapter contributed to your learning?

Please use the space below to record your thoughts.

Dialogic Activity:

- In what ways do the components in Table 5.2 either confirm or inform your school's current policies and practices with respect to bullying issues?
- What information do you need in order to answer the previous question?
- Where in your school or district would you go to find answers?
- With whom would you need to talk?
- Who in your group is willing to make the needed contacts and to find answers?
- When will you report back to this group?

Each of Chapters 6 through 10 presents an Essential Element of Cultural Proficiency that will serve to inform your personal growth and school commitment to reducing and eliminating bullying, with particular emphasis on LGBT students, employees, and community members. Chapter 6 presents Assessing Cultural Knowledge in a way that guides a personal exploration of your knowledge and reaction to LGBT topics, a scan of your school with regard to LGBT issues, and the beginning of personal and institutional commitments to being an even more inclusive school/district.

6 Assessing Cultural Knowledge

It is clear we have an issue (teen LGBT suicides) in our society that needs to be changed, and those of us who are fortunate enough to call education our career can help change it.

—Peter M. DeWitt (2012, p. 3)

> **Assess Culture:** Listen to self to accurately assess what you know about yourself in relation to lesbian, gay, bisexual, and transgender (LGBT) communities. Next, listen to your colleagues as they describe their personal stories, concerns, and attitudes about sexual orientation and gender identity. The ability to assess your own, your colleagues', and your school's cultural knowledge provides important information about the extent to which you facilitate or impede inclusivity.

GETTING CENTERED

Take a few minutes to think about these prompts and respond in the space below:

- How many LGBT faculty and staff do you have at your school?
  - How do you know?
  - How might you find out?
- Are you aware of the age at which straight children know they are straight?

- How is their heterosexuality manifested?
- When did you become conscious of your sexual orientation?
- How are you feeling as you read these questions?

Take a few minutes to write about your feelings, reactions, and thoughts related to these questions.

_____

_____

_____

_____

ASSESSING CULTURAL KNOWLEDGE

The Essential Elements of Cultural Proficiency provide standards and guidelines for planning, evaluating, and implementing policies, practices, and behaviors. Assessing cultural knowledge means that educators must be aware of the overt cultural norms of their school and community and pay attention to the unwritten rules (i.e., the hidden curriculum) that reflects values and norms that may be unstated but pervasive within the school culture. Since attacking members of the LGBT community is often sanctioned, with both overt aggression and micro-assaults, educators who seek to nurture a culturally proficient community must proactively lead community members away from culturally destructive behaviors. This chapter identifies and describes strategies for assessing the culture of your environments. We begin with a case story to illustrate the importance of district leaders' establishing an inclusive and supportive educational environment in which all members feel safe to be who they are and are able to grow and learn.

The Case Story Setting

Westfield Unified School District (WUSD) is located within the greater metro area and serves approximately 24,000 students. The student demographics are composed of 42% white students, 30% Hispanic students, 15% African American students, 10% Asian American students, and 5% Middle Eastern students. The school district is one of the most diverse in the state and has demonstrated that diversity is an asset rather than a problem. Statewide assessment and accountability goals have been set, and expectations are high for all students in the district, including high performance expectations for low socioeconomic student groups. The

English learning students have been transitioning into English proficient levels at an appropriate pace for only the past two years. However, special education students are being served disproportionately compared with the demographic groups represented in the district. The educational gap is closing for some students, wherease for other student groups in the district, the gap-closing strategies are not as effective. The most obvious gap is evident between students who live on the "hill side" of Westfield and those who live in the "flats." The superintendent and his leadership team have taken on the obvious, but rarely talked-about, assumption of WUSD: Where students reside seems to indicate their level of academic achievement, or as one teacher so clearly put it, "Where you live determines what you learn."

Generally speaking, however, overall students success throughout the district has caught the attention of the local community college and area businesses. The area Chamber of Commerce prides itself in the ethnic diversity of the community and has attracted new businesses based on the add campaign, "We are proud of our differences. Come join us!"

WUSD attributes most of the success of closing a long-time achievement gap to a visionary superintendent and a supportive Board of Trustees. Superintendent Mark Charlton joined WUSD five years ago. He came from out of state, having served as superintendent of a similar-sized inner-suburban district. He had earned the reputation of turning around the district from one of where students were being underserved to one where students were served differently, in ways that met their academic and social needs. At his interviews with WUSD teachers, administrators, community members, and board members, Dr. Charlton indicated clearly that he would lead using the Tools of Cultural Proficiency. The board knew when they offered him a contract that he was a man focused on creating equitable schools through collaborative and inclusive leadership practices. At his first leadership retreat with his leadership team, Dr. Charlton emphasized again the use of the Tools of Cultural Proficiency as an approach for closing the educational gaps that had existed at WUSD for many years. Students and their families and community members were enthused to hear him describe how they, too, would be involved and engaged in educating all children and youth of the community. Within the first year of Dr. Charlton's arrival, the community could feel, see, and hear a difference throughout the community. By the end of the fourth year, significant changes in student achievement proved that Dr. Charlton, the teachers, administrators, and staff members were well on their way toward educating all children to levels higher than ever before.

In the summer of Dr. Charlton's fifth year, he began to reflect over the past year and think about several incidents that had occurred in neighboring districts. He also realized that similar events had occurred nationally. These events involved student suicides resulting from incidents of bullying, court cases about students' rights and freedom of speech, conflicts between churches and community gay-straight alliances and organizations, and non-traditional identification of families and extended families. Many of these events were related to students' and family members' sexual identities and orientations or perceived orientations by others who targeted them by bulling or harassing them. These events weighed heavily on Mark's heart. He gathered his leadership team for a two-day retreat to study the district's culture and climate for managing the dynamics of differences about sexual orientations and identity.

Dr. Charlton's approach for facilitating the retreat included an intentional discussion using the lens of Cultural Proficiency. He felt the team needed time to talk and listen to each other. The discussions were structured around the following guiding questions:

- When it comes to creating and supporting a teaching and learning environment for gay, lesbian, bisexual, and transgender people (students and adults) in our district, what assumptions are we holding?
- Who are we listening to and what are we hearing?
- From whom have we not heard?
- What are we noticing?
- What do the data tell us?
- What research do we need to know more about?
- Of what should be aware?
- What barriers might be in our way?
- How might the Guiding Principles inform us?
- How might the five Essential Elements guide our work?

Mark informed the Board of Trustees of the retreat plans and outcomes. All trustees were supportive of Mark's leadership, but two members cautioned Mark that LGBT issues might be too sensitive for some parents to understand. Mark explained that he and the leadership team were willing to face all areas of diversity, not just the more comfortable ones. He shared national data on student suicides, harassment, and verbal and physical assaults. He wanted to make certain students and families in WUSD experience a safe place for their education, regardless of their race, gender, religion, socioeconomic status, or sexual orientation. The board agreed.

Dr. Charlton: *Now, let's get started with what we need to know about our own students. Are our students being harassed because of who they are? Do our students feel safe?*

Ed Walters: *About 10 years ago when I was Director of Student Services we conducted a school climate survey. Things have changed a lot since then. Maybe we should conduct another survey.*

Dr. Charlton: *That's a good place to start Ed. Now that you are Deputy Superintendent, why don't you look into working with our principals to conduct a districtwide, safe schools survey? Let's get new data. This step certainly fits with the Essential Element of assessing cultural knowledge in our Cultural Proficiency plan from our retreat work.*

Reflection

- What do you think about this conversation?
- What might be some other steps the leadership team can take at this stage?
- Why might the board members be cautious at this point in the conversation?

_____

_____

_____

_____

What to Look and Listen For

Scanning and assessing an environment for knowledge of ethnic diversity can be somewhat different from assessing for individuals' and schools' knowledge about sexual orientation. While both are often supported by deeply held beliefs and values about the "other," sexual orienation cuts across ethnic, racial, social class, religious, and ability lines. Learning about people's levels of knowledge about sexual orientation requires vigilant attention to subtleties. If you listen to comments that people make, you will have a better sense of their values toward LGBT communities that may inhibit or facilitate their learning.

Monitoring the environment for language and policies that would make it uncomfortable or unsafe for LGBT people to make themselves known is the role of everyone in the organization. Historically, discrimination and fear have kept many in the LGBT community silent and invisible. Just as you have probably learned to notice discriminatory attitudes directed at women or people of color, you can train yourself to listen to your colleagues to hear their concerns, biases, and attitudes toward sexual orientation differences.

Pay attention to the way language is used. Do you hear blatant comments such as, "God made Adam and Eve, not Adam and Steve"? Do you hear other comments such as, "We know why she isn't married." Do you hear jokes that make fun of LGBT people? When someone speaks up for inclusive language, such as "We're inviting partners as well as spouses, are we not?" do people protest? How often do you hear "that's so gay" used as a putdown by students or your colleagues? These are indications that people either do not know the correct terminology or they harbor culturally incompetent attitudes toward LGBT people. Often these subtle micro-aggressions are more harmful than overt gay bashing, because it is easy to overlook or dismiss a micro-assault. Many times, when people speak out against these comments, the response is, "Don't be so sensitive." Or "No one meant any harm."

Following Superintendent Charlton's Board and Leadership Team Retreat, he and Ed met with five site administrators to begin planning for the culturally proficient "safe place" plan for the district. Mark, the superintendent, and Ed, were surprised by responses from several of the administrators.

Cynthia: *Mark, I appreciate your efforts toward safer schools, but we are in good shape at the elementary school. I know you're worried about the gay kids, but that kind of stuff doesn't happen at the younger ages. We focus on "be kind to each other" and the parents are good with that.*

Marco: *So how's that working out for you, Cyn? I noticed you had an increase in fights on your campus last semester. What's up with that? Little kids not being so kind these days?*

Cynthia: *That's not funny, Marco. We've had a lot of new kids move in and we're trying to bring them up to speed. Nothing about bullying, though. I told you we don't have gay kids in elementary school!*

Angela: *Well, we certainly do at our elementary school, and they get harassed everyday! Cyn, you must not be paying attention to students who may need your help. Watch for kids who others make fun of because of the way they dress and sound or who their friends are. They are called terrible names all the time and are left to play by themselves. Also, watch for kids who have gay or lesbian parents. Other kids are confused by that, too.*

Cynthia: *You have to be kidding, Ange. That's just kids being kids. I can't patrol that kind of behavior. I tell those kids to just be tougher and stronger and ignore those other kids.*

Benjamin: *You can't let that kind of stuff go on at the younger ages. That's why we have such major problems at the high school then. Bullies know they can get away with that stuff 'cause no body is gonna* *report them. We have a great antibullying program at our school, but a lot of victims slip through the cracks because they have spent years being bullied and nobody listens to them. They are alone. Believe me, I know how that feels. Nobody listened to me when I was being bullied in high school. And, yes, Cynthia, I knew I was gay when I was in the fourth grade.*

Dr. Charlton: *As I listen to you, I realize each of you comes to this conversation from your own life experiences. I also realize as a district, we need to take action as a leadership team to assess our own knowledge of our team, our school data, and our resources. Creating a safe place for us to have these conversations is part of our planning as well. If we don't feel safe and knowledgeable, then we can't create a safe place for our students and employees.*

Reflection

Take a few minutes and think about the following questions:

- What are some of the assumptions held by the group members?
- What might be some questions the members can ask each other to assess cultural knowledge?
- In what ways might Dr. Charlton move the group forward to the next steps in their planning?
- Write your responses in the following space.

_____

_____

_____

_____

When assessing the culture of your school and classroom, notice if the language of your colleagues or students is a reflection of their discomfort, their embarrassment, or their values. Sometimes, especially in the precompetent phase, people want to do the right thing but simply do not know what to do. Gently offering appropriate language as an alternative to overt and indirect slurs is very helpful. Often, comments are made out of ignorance and fear. You can often stop such conversations by asking questions or making statements such as these:

- Why would you say that? Are you aware of how that comment might make others feel?
- Well, that hasn't been my experience.

- Is that comment a lack of value you hold for gay students or are you just uncomfortable when they are in your classroom?
- When you say, "those kids" who exactly are you speaking about?
- What might be some reasons you feel our gay and lesbian students don't deserve our best teaching?

These questions help break through the barriers of deeply held assumptions, values, and beliefs that some people are not even aware they are holding on to. Your questions help them assess where they are in their own thinking and help you assess where you are in your own growth in confronting the barriers with inquiry.

LISTEN TO SELF

So who are you? Assessing cultural knowledge is about assessing your own values, beliefs, assumptions, and actions. What is your sexual orientation? When did you first become aware of your sexual orientation? How do you relate to others who have a different sexual orientation than you? A colleague of one of the authors once said,

> I remember the time I finally said the word *gay* aloud. Nothing happened. I thought it would; but nothing happened. I'm not gay, and I couldn't even say the words, *gay* or *lesbian*, much less, *bisexual* or *transgender*. To be able to have conversations at my school and be helpful to anyone else, I had to practice saying these words aloud, in private, first. Strange, I know, but that's how scared I was to admit I didn't know much about the LGBT communities.

This colleague's story is an example of assessing one's culture and being willing to start where you are and move forward.

GOING DEEPER

Personal Reflection: Take a moment to think about these questions:

- What do you think you have missed in your classroom? At your school? In yourself?
- Why do you think you have missed those things?
- So what does it take to abide by district policies that conflict with your personal values?

Use the space below to record your responses. And over the next week listen through the filter of Cultural Proficiency to hear signs and indicators of situations regarding LGBT children that may need your attention.

_____

_____

_____

_____

Dialogic Activity: Talk with a few trusted colleagues and see if you and they know children in your school who are probably gay.

- How do you know?
- Do you know who on your staff is gay?
- Do you know who is straight?
- How do you know?
- Why is it important to know?
- Describe the language or jokes or passing remarks made in your presence that may indicate to the LGBT community at your school that it is safe—or unsafe—to be out about one's sexuality.
- What are policies, if any, about the treatment of LGBT students in your district?
- What policies might affect the LGBT adults in your district? Does the antibullying policy include specific language against bullying people because of their sexual orientation?

Use the space below to record your responses.

_____

_____

_____

_____

_____

_____

As educators, you may never know all that is going on in the life of a student or a faculty or staff member. However, remaining vigilant is critical so that if something is happening in their lives that affects their school experience, you will notice. *Assessing culture* means to know your environment and to pay attention to changes in it. When students become agitated or withdrawn, you can express concern and curiosity. If you do not feel qualified to respond to their needs, know when to offer professional help.

Parents, Families and Friends of Lesbians and Gays (PFLAG; www .pflag.org) is just one resource that is useful for educators and the families of LGBT students. This story is from their files:

> Forty years ago, Queens, New York schoolteacher Jeanne Manford marched with her gay son, Morty, in New York's Christopher Street Liberation Day Parade carrying a sign that read "Parents of Gays Unite in Support for Our Children." She took this historic step after learning of an assault on his life due to his sexual orientation, while police stood by and did nothing to help him. The response to Manford's public support of her son was overwhelming and she was begged by parade participants to speak to other parents and families. Through the next year, this grassroots family and ally movement spread like wildfire and in 1973 Manford, along with a small group of dedicated parents, founded PFLAG, an organization for parents, families, friends, and straight allies to unite with LGBT people in a shared mission of support, education, and advocacy. That this movement spread so quickly—long before the age of the Internet and mobile phones—was clear evidence of the need for this organization, the first and only of its kind. (from the PFLAG.org Home Page, October 2012)

In the Resource D section of this book, we have included references for articles, books, and videos, as well as opportunities for activism and community organizing around the issues of justice for LGBT people. You may find these resources particularly useful as you move into unfamiliar and uncharted areas of sexuality. In a culture that is still uncomfortable with openly discussing sexuality, discussing issues around LGBT lives can be very difficult.

The first step for assessing cultural knowledge is becoming aware of what is around you. In the next chapter, you will learn what it takes to move from awareness of difference to valuing that difference.

7 Valuing Diversity

Don't tell me what you value; tell me what you do and I will tell you what you value.

—Source unknown

> **Value Diversity:** Model inclusive language and practices as a way to let people know your organization is a safe environment. Use terms that reflect your knowledge of and comfort with lesbian, gay, bisexual, and transgender (LGBT) communities.

GETTING CENTERED

Take a moment to think about these questions:

- What does it mean to be tolerant of those who are different from you?
- What does it mean to respect those who are different from you?
- What does it mean to value those who are different from you?
- In what ways do tolerance, respect, and value hold similar and/or different meanings for you?

_____

_____

_____

_____

This chapter presents the second of the Essential Elements, valuing diversity. As authors we have always honored and, yet differentiated among, the three terms *tolerance, respect,* and *value.* We have held valuing difference to a higher status. Tolerance and respect are important concepts that can lead to valuing. Tolerance and respect are states of mind integral to the more proactive behavior demonstrating worth or importance. In the lexicon of Cultural Proficiency, people have to actually *do* something to demonstrate a value for those culturally different from them. In other words, in what ways do you demonstrate the value you hold for those different from you?

Many of us are able to live day-to-day having very little meaningful interaction with persons who are culturally different from us. Stop! Stop for a moment to reread the previous sentence and dwell on the phrase "are able to live." Think about the power of that phrase. For many of us, we live and work each day unaware of the culture of the people with whom we work. Or could there be another explanation when it comes to the difference that is sexual orientation. Could it be that there are those whose sexual orientation or gender diversity is invisible to us, and because of our perceived indifference, these colleagues are uncomfortable sharing their cultures in the workplace? If colleagues might be discomfited, can you imagine what it might be like for our students who are expected to hide their sexual orientation? Yes, maybe the same can be said for religious and social class difference being somewhat invisible, but as you now know, our emphasis in this book is about sexual orientation and, with this chapter, the extent to which we value such difference.

Our experience working with the Tools of Cultural Proficiency has taught us that the Essential Element, *valuing diversity,* is made up of interactive components grounded in advocacy. When we value diversity, we place ourselves as continuous learners committed to living what we believe are in the best interests of a socially just society. Other aspects of valuing diversity include the following four components:

- *Valuing diversity is seeking opportunities for meaningful interactions with those culturally different from us.* Meaningful interactions are those personal and organizational opportunities for developing relationships that lead to knowing, understanding, and valuing another person's culture. Developing cross-cultural relationships begins with our taking the initiative to learn and understand about each other. Often, due to societal and organizational sanctions, many people who are culturally different from the mainstream institutional culture may not initiate meaningful interactions with others for fear of rejection or worse.

Culturally proficient individuals and organizations who value cultural difference must be willing, and in some cases courageous, to initiate meaningful communications and contact. Such contact may begin with a simple personal introductory greeting and progress to immersing one's self in another's cultural milieu. However, caution must be given, that because of the other person's history with organizations such as yours, a risk of rejection or denial of the opportunity to have a meaningful dialogue or other interaction may get in the way. In too many cases, such rejection often leads people to warily stop being proactive. However, culturally proficient people display valuing diversity through demonstrating a persistence in their own continuous learning and advocacy as an aspect of proactivity.

Also important to note is that persistence in pursuit of continuous learning and advocacy has as its goal the improvement of the culture of the organization, not necessarily the short-term approval of those who have been marginalized. LGBT people, in particular, have too often experienced being exploited by people of seeming goodwill who crumbled in the face of push back from their colleagues. People who value diversity demonstrate their value for diversity through advocacy not only when LGBT people are in the room but also, and even more important, when their audience is assumed to be heterosexual.

- *One striving to be culturally proficient takes proactivity to another level by demonstrating a value for diversity in regard to those who are culturally similar to you.* In doing so, another component of valuing diversity is to examine the language and behaviors of those around you. To what extent do your colleagues use offensive, derogatory terms and slurs that target, knowingly or unknowingly, members of the LGBT community? When you hear such comments do you challenge them and indicate your discomfort or displeasure? Are there behaviors or actions that you are aware of that exclude members of the LGBT community in your school/workplace? If so, do you speak up and challenge these behaviors or actions in ways that can be heard and understood? Are you willing to say, "That action/behavior makes me uncomfortable," or "That action/behavior is offensive to me?" Actions such as these often involve risk taking and courage to be forthright, especially when speaking with or confronting coworkers, friends, and/or family members.

- *Valuing diversity entails advocacy in examining institutional policies and practices for their impact on cultural communities.* What policies, practices, and/or procedures are in place in your school/workplace that value or demean cultural groups? To what extent are you aware of the impact of current policies and practices that either demonstrate support for or negatively affect members of the LGBT communities?

Are leaves-of-absence afforded same-sex partners in the same way family leaves-of-absence are awarded to heterosexual partners? Are students welcomed into extracurricular activities traditionally reserved for heterosexual students, such as cheerleading, athletics, homecoming and prom royalty, or student governance? Are there other forms of formal or informal sanctions that might be imposed if a LGBT member were to come out at your school/workplace? The culturally proficient leader proactively reviews all institutional policies to ensure that any vestiges of bias toward LGBT members are removed. The culturally proficient leader also vigilantly ensures that equitable policies are followed by equitable day-to-day practices.

Culturally proficient leaders support equitable policies and practice through sharpening their listening skills. They must not only seek to hear intentional slurs and other derogatory remarks but also be sensitive to subtle and sometimes unintended offensive comments. Listening also presumes that the leader is familiar with expressions that could be deemed offensive and understands the impact of such expressions. We, the authors, have visited schools where educators and students alike reported one of the often-used words was *gay*. Everyone, students, faculty, staff, and community members used the term pejoratively seemingly unaware that it might be offensive to some students or adults. The culturally competent proficient leader must be able to explain that although we certainly live in a society that believes in free speech, we also live in a society where we believe in sharing civility with all members of our collective and diverse communities.

- *Proactivity also has an educative function that extends into the heart and soul of why schools exist—namely, the developing of a literate populace.* The culturally proficient leader extends his or her learning by posing questions that guide us in examining our basic curriculum and instruction. Do our curricula represent LGBT contributions in ways that are natural and normal in our academic disciplines? Are LGBT people who have made major contributions to our nation and the world community duly recognized in our curricula? Do we show the efforts of prominent social justice leaders of the last two generations and how their efforts have led to our curricula expansion now highlighting notables formerly rendered invisible? Today, our school curricula increasingly feature African American, women, Native American/First Nations, Latino/as, and Asian/Pacific Island members along with distinct groups that include religious and national origin identity. Culturally proficient leaders recognize that being silent on identifying notable members of the LGBT community is a form of devaluing rather than valuing. Through our staff development programs, book studies, and other forms of continuous learning, we can provide information and pedaglogical approaches that can be used effectively with students when addressing LGBT content and issues. Knowledge is a very powerful tool for overcoming bias, misinformation, and fears about the "other."

WESTFIELD UNIFIED SCHOOL DISTRICT CASE STORY

Anthony is a 14-year-old student in WUSD's Park Hill Academy, the charter school with a special program for gifted students. He maintains a 3.8 grade point average and is active in many school activities, with particular interest in the swim team and drama club. Through the drama club, he meets another male student, Greg, who becomes his best friend. Anthony's father Javier Jimenez is a first-generation Mexican American. He attended a local high school and married his high school girlfriend Hortencia after they graduated. He is a machinist, and one of his favorite activities includes restoring old cars. Hortencia, who was born in Mexico, recently passed away from breast cancer.

Javier is close to his brothers and sisters and relies on their assistance in helping to raise Anthony. Javier is active with local Chicano organizations and has a circle of male friends with whom he socializes and plays soccer. Most of his male friends are married and have kids. Javier and Anthony live in the same community as Javier's circle of friends and relatives. This is the same area in which Javier grew up and is the neighborhood that his parents lived in when they were alive.

Greg's parents sent him to the Park Hill Academy Charter School because of its diversity and academic reputation. They wanted him to be exposed to different cultures and were excited when he became friends with Anthony. When he was 12, Greg told his parents that he was gay, and the family accepted his sexual orientation without question. Anthony is also gay, but he hasn't told anyone but Greg. He is afraid to talk with his father because his father is so macho. One day, Anthony's father, Javier, discovers several photos of Anthony and Greg. In one photo Greg is kissing Anthony on the cheek. Javier is angry and confronts Anthony.

Javier: *Are you a maricon? Who is this in the picture with you?*

Anthony: *He is Greg, my best friend, Papa.*

Javier: *Not anymore. You will never see him again. He is not welcome in this house! I will go to your school tomorrow and make sure you do not associate with him at school! This is a family disgrace!*

When Javier tells his brother, Anthony's Uncle Miguel, about his discovery Miguel tries to calm Javier and suggests he go talk with one of Anthony's teachers or the counselor at school. Miguel begs his brother to see his son in the same loving way that he has always seen him. Miguel addresses his brother with a plea from his heart.

Miguel: *Maybe we are the ones who need help, not Anthony. Maybe we need to get help from school people so they can help our family.*

Reflection

- What would you do if Javier Jimenez came to talk with you about his son, Anthony?
- Can you say what the attitude toward the LGBT community is in your school? Your neighborhood?
- Can you describe or predict the response toward the LGBT community or individual needs at your school? In your district?

_____

_____

_____

_____

The Story Continues . . .

Javier goes to the school and talks with the principal, Mrs. DuBinion. He shows Mrs. DuBinion the picture and tells her that he does not want Anthony associating with Greg. Mrs. DuBinion tells Javier that Anthony and Greg are just good friends and the picture does not signify anything. She assures Javier that Anthony and Greg are very good students and their friendship is very good for both of them. She also tells Javier that she will make herself available to talk with Anthony to see if he needs help in any way. She reminds Javier that he can come to school anytime for conversations with her, Anthony's teachers, or the counselor.

When Javier returns home, he confronts his son once again.

Javier: *Anthony, tell me now . . . are you . . . gay?*

Anthony: *Yes, Papa, I think I am. And I really like Greg.*

Javier: *I'm sorry for you, Son. I cannot have you live here!*

That night, Anthony leaves home and goes to Greg's house. Greg's parents welcome Anthony and allow him to stay at their home. The parents encourage Anthony and Greg to study together and they talk with Anthony and Greg about the importance of friendships. At school Anthony is sullen, and his principal, Mrs. DuBinion notices Anthony is not his usual self. She asks Mr. Bradley, the school counselor, to talk with Anthony.

Mr. Bradley: *What's going on, Anthony. You seem really unhappy these days.*

Anthony: *I'm confused. I thought my father loved me. He kicked me out of the house because I'm gay. I don't know what to do. I just want to go home and be with my family. I want them to love me for who I am.*

After learning that Anthony was no longer in his home, Mrs. DuBinion called Anthony's father. Mr. Jimenez is unapologetic about his role in Anthony leaving home.

Javier: *Chicano kids do not grow up gay. Anthony is my only son, and I want him to give me grandchildren.*

Mrs. DuBinion: *Mr. Jimenez, I assure you the most important thing is that Anthony remain healthy and do well in school. You may think this is a phase he is going through or just an infatuation with Greg. As parents, we all need help sometimes. Several organizations assist parents of gay children. My friend Rosa contacted an organization called PFLAG. She was able to talk with other Latino parents about her situation. I'll give you some phone numbers and information. And remember, we are here for Anthony and you. We know you care for each other very much.*

In this story, the principal demonstrated a value for cultural differences. She knew the father and son were in conflict about family values that hurt their relationship deeply. The principal stayed in contact with the father and offered the student and the family resources available to them from the school.

GOING DEEPER

Personal Reflection: Take a few minutes to think about these questions:

- In what ways do you demonstrate your value for those different from you?
- Do you know gay "couples" at your school?

- How are they valued or treated?
- What are you learning about yourself as an educator as you read this chapter?

Please use the space below to record your thoughts, feelings, and questions.

_____

_____

_____

_____

Dialogic Activity: Washington State Senator Mary Margaret Haugen had her moral framework challenged when she had to vote for or against legalizing gay marriage in the state of Washington. We include it here and invite you, either alone or with colleagues, to discuss the moral dilemma posed in her decision. Our opinion is that, similar to Sen. Haugen, we as educators must confront the marginalization of LGBT students, family/community, and educators as a test of our moral compass.

> *I have very strong Christian beliefs, and personally I have always said when I accepted the Lord, I became more tolerant of others. I stopped judging people and try to live by the Golden Rule. This is part of my decision. I do not believe it is my role to judge others, regardless of my personal beliefs. It is not always easy to do that. For me personally, I have always believed in traditional marriage between a man and a woman. That is what I believe to this day. But this issue isn't about just what I believe. It's about respecting others, including people who may believe differently than I. It's about whether everyone has the same opportunities for love and companionship and family and security that I have enjoyed.*

> —Washington State Senator Mary Margaret Haugen
> ("Faith-Based Tolerance," 2012)

What thoughts and feelings occur to you as you read the passage? What questions do you pose to yourself? What questions do you pose to your colleagues? What questions do you pose to your school district and your profession? In what ways does Senator Haugen's dilemma parallel that of Javier Jimenez? Please use the space below to record your thoughts, feelings, and questions.

_____

_____

_____

_____

You now have information about becoming aware of your culture and what it means to value culture. In the next chapter, you learn about managing the dynamics of difference when cultures come together in the school setting.

8 Managing the Dynamics of Difference

Inclusion is not bringing people into what already exists; it is making a new space, a better space for everyone.

—George Dei (cited in Ontario Ministry of Education, 2009, p. 4)

> **Manage the Dynamics of Difference:** Proactively address all levels of conflict as natural and normal events, including micro-aggressions and micro-assaults. State clearly that when personal beliefs clash with the organization's commitment to diversity and equity, the organization's core values are paramount.

GETTING CENTERED

Take a moment and think about the following questions:

- As you seek to respond in increasingly culturally proficient ways with LGBT communities, what is your greatest fear?
- What are your greatest hopes?
- What might be the benefits of diverse communities comprised of lesbians, gay men, bisexual people, transgender people, allies, and straight people?

This chapter focuses on the third Essential Element, managing the dynamics of difference. As you seek to become more culturally proficient in your approaches with lesbian, gay, bisexual, and transgender (LGBT) communities you will encounter conflicts among your colleagues and with the communities you serve. You may also face some conflicts within yourself. The conflicts may emerge from differences in religious perspectives, the desire to minimize the issues around LGBT people, heterosexism, and fear. This chapter discusses these conflict areas and suggests approaches for addressing them.

WESTFIELD UNIFIED SCHOOL DISTRICT CASE STORY

As you read the case story, notice if any part of this story resonates with your story.

Dr. Creola Lee DuBinion, principal in WUSD, was raised in a fundamentalist Christian family. They went to church every Sunday morning and on Wednesday evening of every week. The church was founded by Creola's great grandfather and pastored in succession by her grandfather and her uncle. Creola met her husband, Michael Robinson DuBinion, coach at the high school and sponsor of the Jazz Club, at church. Michael and Creola have raised their children, who are now in college, in this same church. Church means family, community, spiritual life, and social life for Creola.

Creola currently serves as the Sunday School Superintendent, responsible for the Christian Education for all the children and adults in the church. She enjoys teaching junior high youth. This role has given her firsthand experience with the young people, which she has missed since becoming principal at the school where she was a teacher. One of the ministries that emerged from the Christian Education department is Return to the Image. This ministry is for homosexuals who seek to return to the image of God in which they believe they were created and to the traditional roles of men and women as they believe were ordained by God.

Creola and her husband recently returned from a three-year stay in Boston where Creola attended Boston University and earned her doctorate in education. At the university she was exposed to people from all over the world. She and her family enjoyed living in a large metropolitan area for the cultural opportunities they experienced. Her dissertation research looked at how the lens of cultural proficiency shaped educational leadership. As she went deeper into her studies, Creola began to see that the values with which she was raised, while appropriate for her and her family, might not similarly serve all the children in her school or their families.

When she returned to the district after her sabbatical leave, with her diploma in hand, Creola was placed as principal at Park Hill Academy in an economically comfortable neighborhood. Recently, incidents of bullying increased. The school implemented an antibullying program. The district established a team to study its policies on LGBT students and bullying. The superintendent, Dr. Charlton, and the Board of Education have already made it clear that the rights of gay students and educators need to be protected. This is not the most comfortable place to be for Creola. The Christian values with which she was raised are being challenged, but she knows she must keep her students and employees safe. Her neatly organized life is starting to be tested at the core.

At the faculty meeting in September:

Mrs. DuBinion: *We are welcoming a new student to our school next week. This is a transgender girl, Daniella, for whom we will need to make a few special accommodations. I've provided you with a glossary of terms that we will use as we discuss the educational needs of this child. First of all, Daniella IS a GIRL. She is not a he/she; she is not a boy. She identifies as a girl, and is wearing girl's clothes. Medically speaking, she has not had any gender reassignment surgery, which means that on the outside, her genitalia are that of a boy. For this reason, she will be using the single restroom in the Health Office on the main hall.*

Mrs. Anderson: *That's close to my room. It's usually an adult restroom. Kids are gonna ask why she is using that restroom. What do we say?*

Mrs. DuBinion: *Well, I'd like to tell them it's none of their business (nervous laughter, from everyone), but instead tell them, that Daniella's parents want her to use a private restroom. If the kids push, say it is a private issue. The resource teachers are working with Daniella and her social worker so that she, too, has appropriate responses to the curious questions of students. Also, she will not take a PE class this first semester. If kids ask, tell them she has a doctor's excuse just like many other students do—which is accurate. She is in the Explorer Band class and advanced art class for her electives. She is extremely bright and talented, and we want her to have an excellent school year at Park Hill School.*

Three weeks later, Mrs. DuBinion had a conversation with three students.

Freddie: *My mom told me not to go near that boy/girl.*

Angela: *Freddie, you don't go around most girls anyway! Mrs. DuBinion, my parents are upset, too. I want to be her friend, but they said to wait and see what everyone else does.*

Tres: *Mrs. DuBinion, what about the stuff we studied in our class at church? Pastor Harold says what she did is wrong. My folks won't even let me talk about that stuff at home. I told them that some gay people did some really great things, like we studied in class. They don't want to hear it. I think I get it, though.*

Mrs. DuBinion: *Well, Freddie, I know that your parents told you not to associate with Daniella; I have spoken to them. Daniella is not gay, she is transgender. You do not have to be friends with Daniella, but your parents understand that as long as you are in this school, you will speak politely and if you end up next to her for any reason, you will remain where you are and treat her respectfully, just like we do all students here at West Middle.*

Angela, why don't you come with me and I will introduce you to Daniella and her friends.

Tres, let's talk at church next Wednesday evening about some of your ideas. I've been doing some thinking, too.

RELIGION

Many religious leaders teach that homosexuality is a sin. Our intention as authors of this book is not to dissuade you, the reader, from any religious doctrine. Our intention is to clearly state what is appropriate behavior and language in a school setting. In cases where believers are taught that homosexuality is wrong, the corollary teaching, usually, is "to hate the sin, not the sinner." Moreover, since almost every theological and spiritual tradition has a version of what is commonly called "The Golden Rule," which admonishes the spiritual sojourner to treat others with kindness and respect, as they would like to be treated, religious conflicts can be addressed, in part, by asking believers to treat LGBT adults and children with kindness.

Some argue that educators are being asked to teach their students, faculty, or staff how to be members of the LGBT community, or contrary to their religious beliefs, to teach that being LGBT is socially acceptable. However, that is not the case. Recent policies and practices to include the contributions of LGBT Americans in the curriculum do not mean that educators are required to teach people to be gay. Educators are being asked to teach that the LGBT community *exists* and that minimally, as a minority group that has historically been targeted for culturally destructive behavior, its members require civility and respect, and in the case of children, protection from isolation, discrimination, hostility, bullying, and micro-assaults. Just as religious teachings were used to discourage the integration of African American children and the equal treatment of women, this is an issue where religion and society may clash. It is important to note, at the same time, that other church leaders have used religious teachings to promote civil rights for African Americans and women, in particular, and for human rights for all cultural groups. Treating LGBT community members with respect and providing them protection and safe places are issues where educators are called to balance their adherence to religious teachings with their compliance to the legal, regulatory, and ethical statutes of the state/province, district/board, and school.

BULLYING TARGETS

The culturally destructive treatment of LGBT children or adults is often minimized by saying the treatment of them falls under the umbrella of bullying. While the mistreatment of members of the LGBT community can be addressed to a minor degree through a blanket program against bullying, we must also understand this is an area of concern far more complex than simply purchasing antibullying programs for schools. As we presented in Chapter 5, although antibullying programs do provide a degree of safety and attention for the school community, much more must be done to address underlying causes of these destructive behaviors by the bullies and the negative environment in which they are allowed to thrive. Managing the dynamics of difference of responses to treatment of members of LGBT communities involves values and beliefs, societal norms and assumptions, socially sanctioned prejudice, and very nontraditional content for the curriculum. Responding to these complex issues requires far more than developing an antibullying program, and to frame it solely as such is to be culturally blind.

TARGETS AND MICRO-AGGRESSIONS AND MICRO-ASSAULTS

Target is another term for identifying those who are the objects of hateful and hurtful comments. A target group is one that the dominant group subjects to various types of harassment and violence. A person who is a target may be a member of a targeted group or may be isolated as an individual for harassment. Classroom teachers can easily identify the kids in their rooms who are targets. The bigger question is, what does the teacher do when those comments are made? The LGBT community is a target group. They are targeted by social groups, media, and individuals. Many members of the LGBT community are often subjected to insults, ridicule, and physical and verbal violence almost everywhere they go. Moreover, in their perceived absence, casual conversation is often peppered with comments that function as micro-assaults against LGBT people. The following paragraphs provide detailed examples based in heterosexism and fear.

Micro-aggressions and micro-assaults are words and actions that when pointed out are too easily dismissed as isolated incidents or oversights that were not meant to harm (Sue, 2010). Micro-assaults hurt and embarrass people. This type of violence never comes as an isolated incident; it comes in a cluster. Throughout the day, a person may experience a number of off-hand remarks, social slights, and small insults masquerading as humor, that cumulatively deliver the message that "this is not a safe place for you," and "we don't respect your kind of people." The culturally proficient educator will raise awareness by responding to these comments and slights every time they occur with responses like these:

"That kind of language is not OK here."

"I know you didn't mean any harm, but making comments like that is hurtful."

"It doesn't matter if you didn't think any gay people were in the room, it is never OK to say things like that in this school."

Sometimes, a culturally proficient educator may find that simply asking a question is helpful: "What did you mean when you said, 'That's so gay'?" It is not, however, helpful to say, "You know George is gay. Don't talk like that around him." Such a comment implies that it is OK to make intolerant remarks when the targeted people are not in the vicinity. Comments like these also give George unwanted and possibly uncomfortable attention, especially if he has not come out to everyone present.

Heterosexism

One of the Guiding Principles of Cultural Proficiency is that the dominant culture serves people to varying degrees. When one person is of the dominant culture, he may find it difficult to see that others do not share the same privileges, power, and access as he does. In schools, all straight educators are in that dominant culture. Often, some members of that dominant culture ask (about LGBT people), "I accept them, but can't they just keep their lifestyle to themselves?" This attitude reflects the mistaken assumption that sexual orientation and gender identity are about sexual acts, and it reflects the privilege of the dominant culture to unconsciously display images and symbols of their lives that LGBT members cannot. For example, it is very common to walk into the office of an educational administrator or resource teacher and see photos of their family—spouse and children. When talking about life outside of school, straight educators speak freely about their husbands and wives, girlfriends and boyfriends. If a spouse visits on campus, it is not deemed unusual or provocative if they touch briefly, hold hands, or exchange a quick kiss. However, these behaviors might be entirely unacceptable behavior for a gay or lesbian couple at many school campuses. Even more unacceptable might be for the gay parents of a student to display these relationship intimacies that are entirely acceptable among members of the dominant culture (i.e., straight couples).

Heterosexism is the belief that straight relationships are the norm *and* are the preferred mode of interacting. As members of a dominant group, heterosexuals have the power to impose their norms on others, to limit their public interaction, and to target LGBT people with micro-assaults and overt policies that marginalize and silence them. A culturally proficient educator understands these power relationships and works to create more equitable environments for the adults and children in the school community. Speaking up when heterosexist attitudes are present in the language of colleagues or the policies of the district requires confidence and a willingness to manage the dynamics of differences in ways that maintain the dignity of all people involved in the situation. Use the opportunity as an education moment to show respect for the lives of all groups. One of our colleagues recently asked, "Why do straight people refer to our 'gay lifestyle,' when really it is our 'life,' just like theirs?

Fear

Even if you do not personally approve of the lives of LGBT people, they do exist, and it is a moral and ethical imperative that if we as educators seek to create an equitable and inclusive learning environment, we acknowledge the diversity of the students and the families they come from. This is not always easy to do. Sister Joan Chittister, Order of St. Benedict (2010), identifies three obstacles to being a moral force in the world: fear of loss of status, personal discomfort, and fear of criticism. The culturally proficient educator must speak up in spite of these fears.

Sometimes, in the precompetence phase of growth, people are fearful they will say the wrong thing or be uncomfortable in the company of gay people or even in discussing LGBT topics and issues. They may attempt to say things that are nice and appropriate so others won't criticize them. Some people may struggle with the language needed to have these conversations. The culturally proficient educational leader can assist teachers, staff members, parents, and students by providing opportunities for conversations using a script giving appropriate information and necessary vocabulary and definitions.

MANAGE THROUGH FACILITATION

Facilitating conversations about LGBT issues requires confidence, compassion, courage, candor, and clarity. Confidence as a facilitator comes with skill and competence. Facilitation skills are developed through training and practice. In Resource D of this book we recommend Adaptive Schools Training and Cognitive Coaching Training along with other training programs designed to enhance conversations about equity and social justice issues. Compassion invites the speakers to be kind to one another and to the subjects of conversation. No name-calling and no slurs are allowed. Clear guidelines and outcomes are set for the conversations. Courage means that often you may be the only one willing to speak up. A culturally proficient educational leader does just that. He speaks up to ensure that the environment is safe and inclusive of everyone. He raises issues that are being ignored, blurred, or otherwise diminished. She is clear that the issue is educational equity, and she helps her colleagues to stay on track with a focused conversation about relevant issues. She manages the dynamics of differences by making space for all voices to be heard. Guiding questions for critical conversations are these: Is it true? Is it kind? Is it necessary? Is this the right time?

The journey toward cultural proficiency often requires a fearless inventory of one's own misperceptions, misjudgments, biases, and fears. Only then can one engage with others in conversations that foster learning, growth, and change in behavior. Conversations, skillfully facilitated, speak the truth when no one can or will. They give voice to the voiceless and speak the truth from the best of oneself to others' best self.

Sometimes the most critical time is spent with children and youth to answer their questions, to reframe their biases, to offer alternatives to their value judgments. At other times, the critical conversations will be with parents: parents who do not understand and or reject their LGBT children, parents who do not want their children exposed to LGBT people, parents who need help in answering their children's questions. Most often, other critical conversations will be with colleagues: colleagues who are gay and closeted, colleagues who are adamantly against a culture that includes LGBT people, and colleagues who need language to engage with their students and colleagues. The goal in each situation is to keep the conversation going, and to keep learning.

GOING DEEPER

Personal Reflection: Think about and respond to these questions:

- As you read this chapter, what personal conflicts or affirmations emerged for you?
- What might be some "dynamics of differences" that you need to manage in your personal and professional lives?
- In what ways has this chapter helped you develop as a culturally proficient educator?

_____

_____

_____

_____

Dialogic Activity: Activities 1 and 2 in Resources C.1 and C.2 may be useful in priming the pump for conversation with your colleagues. The purpose of the activities is to raise awareness of the privilege afforded to members of the dominant culture, which in this case is the culture of heterosexuals. After the members of your group respond to the questions and tally their scores for Activity 2, discuss what those scores mean to you as a professional community learning to be culturally proficient.

You now have information and, hopefully, a degree of mastery with three of the Essential Elements. Chapter 9 is about how you and your school adapt to the diversity of your school in ways that help LGBT colleagues, students, and parents/community members become full participants in the culture of the school.

9 Adapting to Diversity

A positive school culture that is not afraid to address LGBTQ issues can help all students feel accepted, and help our young adults grow as people and as learners.

—Peter M. Dewitt (2012, p. 30)

> **Adapt to Diversity:** Provide professional development for educators that meets the academic and social needs of lesbian, gay, bisexual, and transgender (LGBT) students, faculty and staff, and community members. Develop a culture of holding one another responsible for appropriate language and behavior. Assist colleagues as they adjust to new ideas and ways of supporting LGBT communities.

GETTING CENTERED

Have you found yourself in the faculty/staff room on Monday morning when a colleague started talking about what she and her spouse did over the weekend but quickly changed to talking about the weather instead when she realized one of the gay staff members had entered the conversation?

- How might the conversation have gone if a nonstraight person had described his life away from school?
- How would you have felt if he had described what he and his partner had done over the weekend? What were your assumptions

about what he might say? How might the conversation have gone if you had not known the sexual orientation of all the participants in the conversation?

- How are you feeling as you read these questions?

Take a few minutes to write about your feelings, reactions, and thoughts related to the situation and the questions described here.

_____

_____

_____

_____

ADAPTING TO DIVERSITY WITHIN THE SCHOOL COMMUNITY

What does it mean to adapt to the diversity presented when working with people whose sexual orientation or gender identity is different from yours and your school/district/community, with particular focus on

- students,

- adults; employees of the school/district/agency,

- parents/guardians/foster care providers, and

- institution/school—custodial care of students that interfaces with schools?

The purpose of this chapter is to define and give illustrations to the fourth Essential Element, adapting to diversity. We further describe this Essential Element as "learning about cultural groups different from your own and the ability to use others' cultural experiences and backgrounds in all school settings" (CampbellJones, CampbellJones, & Lindsey, 2010, p. 29). In this book, we give particular attention to a community of adults, employees of school districts, and parents and guardians of the students in that community who are responsible for creating conditions in which all students and adults, especially LGBT people, feel safe and valued as learners. We include adults in this description of "learner" because we approach teaching and parenting as lifelong professions. And we believe we are all in this endeavor of educating our youth, together!

WESTFIELD UNIFIED SCHOOL DISTRICT CASE STORY

Daniel Forester has taught 10th- and 11th-grade English/language arts at the high school for the past twelve years. His colleague, Seth Howard is a 10th-grade social studies teacher and joined the faculty five years earlier. The school counselor, Tisha Jackson, welcomes Seth and Daniel into her office and closes the door. She invites them to join her for coffee or tea and asks Daniel to begin the meeting.

Daniel:	*Thanks so much for meeting with me, Guys. I'm at a loss about what to do in this situation. Just when I think I've heard it all in my 12 years of teaching, this comes up!*
Tisha:	*OK, Daniel, what's this all about? You said you needed to talk, ASAP, to the two of us. So Seth and me? Is this a "gay thing"?*
Seth:	*Well, Tisha, that's certainly being blunt enough. Daniel, what's going on?*
Daniel:	*Yeah, it is a gay thing. We had an English Department meeting this morning. One of the faculty members was talking to a small group of us before the meeting started. He said he called home yesterday to one of his students who was getting behind in his work. The teacher wanted to have a parent conference but was confused about whom to meet with since the kid has, "two moms" and did the quotes-in-the-air-thing. I could tell he was making fun of the student's situation. Then, he said, "The kid seems normal otherwise. So I left a voice message and said, 'I need to have a conference with whichever one of you is Matt's parent.'" I could not believe what I was hearing!! And to add even more shock factor, the other teachers laughed at what he said! What is going on here? I thought we were a progressive school and district. How did we get to this place of not understanding our kids' families any better than this? And to make it worse, I didn't say a word! I was speechless. I am as much to blame as that teacher was! I'm so upset with myself and with him. I just needed to talk with both of you.*
Tisha:	*OK, Daniel, try to calm down a bit. I know you are upset about what happened and what you heard. And you are more upset about what you didn't do.*
Seth:	*Hey, Man. Breathe. You did do something. You heard what the guy said and you got upset. Now, you are telling us, and we are thinking about the situation together. Like the book we are reading, we are reflecting on what happened. So you still have time to think about what you can say to your fellow department member. You could just let it go, but we know you won't do that.*

Tisha: *More kids need teachers like you, Daniel. LGBT kids come to my office often and say how much they appreciate teachers who "get them" without making an issue of their sexual identity. They also know adults here at school who don't "get them." The kids say many adults seem to be afraid of them or don't know what to do with them, so they, those teachers, just ignore them. Like Seth said, you are not willing to let this go, because you know it's really about the kids and their well-being.*

Daniel: *You're right about that. Since we started the cultural proficiency work, I see things differently now. So I guess I thought everyone else would too. You know our last book study and faculty workshops were focused on creating supportive LGBT environments. When our superintendent made this a district priority at the beginning of the year, I thought everyone would reflect on views like I did. Of course, I had the two of you help me examine my own values and beliefs. This recent example just shows me how much work we still have to do—or at least I have to do. I need to know what to say, when I don't know what to say.*

Seth: *Well, that's certainly one way to look at it, Daniel. So let's think about what you might say to that guy in a couple of days when you've cooled down a bit.*

Reflection

As you read the case story, what were you thinking about the interaction of the three adults? What is the role of allies when gay and lesbian people encounter insensitive comments like Daniel did? How might you have reacted if you had been Daniel or Seth or Tisha? What stories do you have to share with your colleagues or students that might be helpful to them as they adapt to personal experiences of others?

_____

_____

_____

_____

ADAPTING TO DIVERSITY

Adapting to diversity means expressing our commitment to teaching the students we have in our classrooms and school rather than the students who used to be here or who we wish were here. Today's classrooms are filled with students of diverse perspectives, learning styles, languages, faiths, physical and mental abilities, life experiences, cultures and ethnicities, sexual orientations, and gender identities. Many educators would have only positive reactions reading this list of diverse descriptors of today's learners. However, some educators would question the inclusion of sexual orientation in the listing of diversity indicators. First, some might say, since sexual orientation is invisible, what difference would that difference make in our classrooms? Second, others might ask, Is sexual orientation considered a cultural difference? Our response to these inquires is simple: The differences are personal and life experiences. Those experiences allow for the individuals' and groups' perspectives, slang expressions, literature, and histories.

Sexual orientation and gender identity as demographic groups possess cultural norms and behaviors as do the racial, ethnic, or faith groups with which they intersect. As educators we view these norms and behaviors not as deficits but as cultural assets learners bring to the school community. This shift in thinking to an "assets" perspective is evident with emerging inclusive norms. Our moral duty as culturally proficient educators is to create safe spaces for students, educators, and parents to be the contribution they want to be (Zander & Zander, 2000).

Taking Time to Adapt and Grow

Culturally proficient educators adapt to changing community needs by setting aside time to do the new work. As you have noted throughout this book, we refer to cultural proficiency as an *inside-out approach* toward advocacy for LGBT learners. The *inside* work is the personal, mindful, reflective thinking and acting in ways that examine your own beliefs, values, and assumptions. These thoughts and actions demonstrate the core values, or Guiding Principles of Cultural Proficiency. Your actions are viewed by others as overcoming barriers that often get in the way of establishing safe and healthy teaching and learning environments. Others see you as an educator or parent who is willing to take time to reflect on your own actions and assume responsibility for your words and deeds, both publically and privately. When leaders set aside time for systemic, continuous, personal and organization growth, members of the organization view the actions of the leaders' commitments of time, people, and resources as a priority for inclusion and equity rather than as a response to a crisis or an afterthought.

Culturally proficient educators use time as an ally by committing organizational resources to support professional learning. Using professional learning to support teachers and parents is one way to use the *outside approach* for developing a culturally proficient educational environment (e.g., reflection time, storytelling, putting into practice new professional development strategies). The awareness of and constructive use of external resources such as community-based events, state-funded projects, and national initiatives position community leaders and educators to be seen as advocates of student needs and community responders. This systemic approach for sharing funding sources to achieve high-priority learning goals for all learners develops and maintains relationships within the school and the community being served by the school.

Supporting All Learners

Educators and parents and guardians of LGBT youth continue to explore ways in which they might work together to create a safe and supportive academic environment for their students and youth. If educators do not address the needs of LGBT learners, then they are not addressing the needs of all learners (Dewitt, 2012). To meet these needs, culturally proficient educators will engage with colleagues to learn to have these planning conversations. One educator told one of our authors this story:

> I worked for several days with a colleague to just say the words *gay* and *lesbian* aloud. He had never said them out loud before. He said he felt unclean just saying them. When I reminded him I am gay, he said, " But, I know you." He just needed to say the words to a person he knew. From there, we were able to have other conversations, and he was able to move forward with conversations in his classroom. We just have to work together and learn from each other.

Many resources are available for educators to guide classroom conversations and develop lesson plans inclusive of LGBT members. Several key resources are included in Resource D.

Culturally proficient educators are mindful of the needs of LGBT students, parents, and school personnel and adapt the teaching and learning environment to create safe places for teachers to teach and students to learn. Specifically, educators, partnering with parents, guardians, foster care providers, and community agencies, can engage in the following culturally proficient activities to adapt to the diversity of their changing communities:

- Purge school forms of heteronormativity (Ask for "parent name" rather than "mother and father" names).
- Adopt "sexual orientation and gender identity or perceived identity," in district antibullying, discrimination, and harassment policies.

- Include sexuality as part of discussions for multiculturalism, diversity, and cultural proficiency.
- Convene a parents-educators-students committee to review and collect literature inclusive of LGBT persons and their histories and contributions, school and family resources, and recommendations for additions to library resources.
- Launch a curriculum review to determine gaps in alignment with Common Core Standards and LGBT persons and their histories and contributions.
- Implement results of curriculum review and make adjustments and additions of LGBT persons and their histories and contributions to the overall curriculum.
- Plan and implement professional learning seminars for educators to include lesson design for new curriculum and conversations.
- Launch an inquiry modeled after the Gay, Lesbian and Straight Education Network school climate survey (Kosciw, Greytak, Bartkiewicz, Boesen, & Palmer, 2012; Kosciw, Greytak, Diaz, & Bartkiewicz, 2010) to gauge student safety perceptions.
- Using survey data from parents and students, plan and implement parent learning seminars with area social and health educators as partners and seminar copresenters.
- Create an environment of professional learning that values storytelling. Teach the value of telling stories in a safe place. Exploring the power of narrative or storytelling is a way to build the foundation for adapting to the diversity of changing communities. Once leaders have built a high value for narrative and are taught the skills of telling and listening, stories become the way to honor differences and grow in new knowledge and new relationships.

Culturally proficient communities are willing to examine their own organizations' values, beliefs, and assumptions found in their stories and their actions. Valuing the diversity within the community and using the assets each member brings will lead to greater adaptation to the changing community.

GOING DEEPER

Personal Reflection: Think about the case story that you read earlier in this chapter. Using the lens of Cultural Proficiency and the Essential Element of adapting to diversity, what might be comments and questions Daniel could say when he confronts his department colleague? In what way might you have responded had you been Daniel? Please use the space below to record your comments.

_____

_____

_____

_____

Dialogic Activity: Engage your colleagues in what adaptation means for the individual educator/staff member and for your school as a whole. What are implications for curriculum, instruction, extracurricular activities, and parent/guardian outreach? The space below is provided to record your findings.

_____

_____

_____

_____

Chapter 10 covers the fifth and final Essential Element—institutionalizing cultural knowledge. You will be able to put into operation the coming together of the Essential Elements in ways that render you and your school effective in responding to the LGBT communities in your school.

10 Institutionalizing Cultural Knowledge

You, Your School, and Your Community

Part of what it means to be a professional, and being a professional educator, is that you are purposely out of step. If you are not out of step, if you are not advocating positions that are in fact different from those of your average parent and the average teacher—then, you are probably not doing your job.

—Lee Shulman (2012, p. 3)

Institutionalize Cultural Knowledge: Engage self and lead colleagues to examine personal beliefs and organizational values that support justice and equity for lesbian, gay, bisexual, and transgender (LGBT) communities. Engage colleagues in conversations to deepen understandings and attitudes of being a diverse and inclusive learning community. Review professional development curricula to ensure inclusivity of topics and issues that affect LGBT colleagues, students, and community members.

GETTING CENTERED

What do we do with what we are learning? Often, learning about and accepting cultural values and behaviors different from our own requires us to *unlearn* or deconstruct our one way of learning or single point of view and to become more aware of different ways of learning and living. When we are open to new ways, different ways, and multiple perspectives, we are more open to surprises and are less likely to experience confusion, fear, and anger in cross-cultural interactions (Vaill, 1966). Individuals who are willing to examine their own values and behaviors along with those of their colleagues collectively within the espoused values of the organization and ask the question, "Are we who we say we are?" are deconstructing their own learning in ways to better align their actions with their vision and core values. This deep, reflective, creative, inside-out process is one way to institutionalize and share cultural knowledge.

Take a few minutes to think about and respond to the following questions:

- In what ways am I deconstructing my learning through the lens of Cultural Proficiency?
- What values have I reexamined about my views toward the LGBT and the straight alliance communities?
- What questions do I still have about who I am within the communities I serve?
- Who are we as an organization?
- Are we who we say we are?

_____

_____

_____

_____

INSTITUTIONALIZING CULTURAL KNOWLEDGE: AN INSIDE-OUT PROCESS

Institutionalizing cultural knowledge is the fifth and final Essential Element of Cultural Competence. A significant feature of institutionalizing cultural knowledge is advocating for and hosting opportunities for sharing expertise to address access opportunities for LGBT students, faculty/staff, and families served by your school. Being an educator committed to institutionalizing cultural knowledge, you intentionally seek input from LGBT communities, with particular attention to those who do not assert their voices or perspectives. Your common frame is to address access and achievement concerns that involve their children. You assess policies and practices to ensure that equitable decisions consider all community members' input, with particular focus on LGBT students.

This chapter is designed to guide you in learning how to institutionalize continuous learning about your own and your school's prevalent beliefs about sexual orientation and gender diversity. You are guided, also, in becoming aware of how your beliefs and behaviors are experienced by others. Once you have engaged in personal reflection and dialogue with your colleagues, you will be well prepared to learn about the manner in which the culture of your school affects the diverse LGBT community you serve.

Institutionalizing cultural knowledge occurs when a school and district holds learning about LGBT communities within the school and its community as core values for ongoing professional learning opportunities. You analyze how institutionalizing cultural knowledge involves school members engaging productively with LGBT communities. Understanding the extent to which cultural knowledge is evident in educator behavior and in school policies and practices equips you to address educational inequities in closing educational access and opportunity and achievement gaps. Data are revealed in ways that cause members of the school community to confront and question issues of disparity of resources, lack of access by some students and their families, and inequity of curriculum and materials. Policies and procedures are then examined to publicly address and correct ongoing concerns about ways to improve learning for all students, with special attention to LGBT students.

Institutionalizing Cultural Knowledge Transforms My Practice

Institutionalizing cultural knowledge for our school and our community begins with developing the capacity to monitor our own cultural knowledge growth and development and being transparent with our actions when working with LGBT communities. Schools and communities that are successful with LGBT students engage in processes of self-reflection to assess their practices and critically reflect on their ideologies, perspectives, beliefs, and attitudes that lead to necessary changes in instruction. Effective schools and communities are well aware that a one-size-fits-all attitude is not the solution.

Institutionalizing Cultural Knowledge Transforms Our School and Community

Reflection and dialogue are indispensable tools in the hands of educators engaged in culturally proficient practices. Reflection on practice is fundamental to transforming and changing our perspectives, as necessary, regarding LGBT students, educators/staff, and our communities (Campos, 2005; DeWitt, 2012). We must be engaged in critically reflective dialogue on how LGBT communities are served as part of a strategic professional learning plan. The professional learning plan must be long term and collaborative and include continuous learning for educators to grow and develop knowledge about the LGBT communities we serve. Additionally, the professional learning plan provides professional resources for LGBT families to address access and achievement parameters for their children. By all stakeholders being engaged in critical dialogue, discourse, and reflection, we can move forward in institutionalizing cultural knowledge that enables school personnel to make equitable decisions.

The Essential Element of institutionalizing cultural knowledge supports our learning about the assets that our LGBT students, colleagues, and families possess in their communities. Through valuing students' assets we can further ensure their academic success to narrow and close the prevalent access and achievement gaps between our LGBT students and all other students. These practices will guide our commitment to equitable access, opportunities, and outcomes for students throughout the school.

MY INSIDE-OUT LEARNING PROCESS

- To what degree am I internalizing the five Essential Elements?
- In what ways can I make these Essential Elements part of my personal and professional practice?
- Now that I know what I know about institutionalizing cultural knowledge, to what learning or action am I willing to commit?

Reflection

_____

_____

_____

_____

Facilitating My School's Inside-Out Learning Process About Institutionalizing Cultural Knowledge

- What are some of the issues facing my school that might be addressed through the Essential Element of institutionalizing cultural knowledge?
- To what degree are we aware of policies and practices that foster the development of programs for LGBT students, faculty/staff, and community members?
- In what ways might we work together to institutionalize culturally proficient practices that serve the needs of our LGBT communities?

Reflection

_____

_____

_____

_____

Facilitating My School's Inside-Out Learning Process About the Communities We Serve

- In what ways might this chapter inform my work with the community our school serves?
- How might I incorporate this chapter's message with our plan for better serving LGBT students, colleagues, and constituents?
- In what ways might we serve and partner with our communities to institutionalize our cultural knowledge in support of all learners?
- What would be some indicators of success that our LGBT students would benefit from culturally proficient practices?

Reflection

_____

_____

_____

_____

WESTFIELD UNIFIED SCHOOL DISTRICT CASE STORY

Superintendent Mark Charlton and the Westfield Unified School District's Leadership Team have spent the school year reviewing the district's policies, procedures, and practices to determine if all students and adults experience a safe and supportive teaching and learning environment. Dr. Charlton and the team gave special attention to the safety of the environments experienced by LGBT students and adults in the district. His goal at the beginning of the year was to provide professional learning experiences for teachers, administrators, staff members, and parents to use the lens of Cultural Proficiency to examine the current teaching and learning environments. He presented the lens of Cultural Proficiency as a way to access the district's cultural knowledge of how LGBT youth and adults were treated and responded to in WUSD schools. Dr. Charlton and the leadership team used the Essential Elements of Cultural Competence as standards of behavior to engage educators, parents, and students in professional practices and schoolwide actions.

Dr. Charlton and his administrative staff kept the school board members informed and involved in this goal-oriented plan throughout the year. Board members were aware of conflicts that arose because of religious views and how school administrators managed those points of conflict in caring and consistent ways. Two board members, Mark Johnston, board president, and Rhonda Thompson a long-time resident of the community had wanted the district to maintain a "low profile" on LGBT issues, especially related to curriculum, bullying, and religious conflicts. Three board members—Barbara Wilson, Tom Turner, and William Stone—had been supportive of the superintendent's goals for equitable, safe, and supportive school environments for all students. While the board members agreed that something more needed to be done, they were not certain how to move forward. Mark, a graduate of the local high school, would like to keep things quiet about any LGBT issues that occur at the school. Barbara, new to the area, holds an executive position at the community's largest corporation. She transferred into the community three years ago with the corporation. She is 39 years old and has never been married.

At a recent board meeting, a group of students from the local high school came to a board meeting and asked if they could have a board-sponsored resolution allowing the establishment of an LGBTSA club at the high school.

Barbara: *Well, students, thank you for bring this suggestion forward to us. This is certainly a worthy request. Let's see, now. LGBTSA? That's Lesbian, Gay, Bisexual, Transgender/Straight Alliance club, right? Have you spoken with your principal, and do you have an adult at the school who has agreed to sponsor the group?*

Mark: *Wait, wait, Ms. Wilson, let's not get ahead of ourselves here. I'm not sure our community is ready for this kind of club (nervous laugh). If you know what I mean. We need to do a little investigating here. We need to talk to the principal and the parents, ourselves . . . uh, the superintendent, uh, the pastors in the community. I mean, you know lots of people before we make this a formal resolution. You know what I mean? This is about homosexuals. Part of our educational responsibility is to teach our students correct moral values.*

Barbara: *I can't believe you just said those things, Mr. Johnston! These students are very smart and brave to come here this evening with this request. As a gay woman I wished that my high school had provided support for me through an LGBT organization. I was confused about my feelings, and I had nowhere to turn, no one to talk with about what I was experiencing. I saw a couple of kids*

> *who others in the school called gay be ridiculed and ostracized, so I stayed in the closet while being in constant fear that someone would find out that I was different. I needed an adult who cared and knew how to help other kids who were bullying us. That is what this club and good information can do for kids today.*

Tom: *This is a serious request and an important conversation. Arguing about this will do our students and families no good. Can we agree to request the superintendent's staff to look into what it would take to establish this club at this school? Does it take our action or is it a school community decision? As community leaders, we need to step up and take a stand on what I think is a social justice issue. We need to ensure that all our students have an environment that is physically, emotionally, and psychologically safe. This can only be accomplished in a school culture that values all forms of differences. This is the Cultural Proficiency lens we have been working on all year. Our leadership will be instructive to our students, faculty, staff, and the larger community. Can we agree to move forward, for the support of our students?*

Although Mark was mostly silent, the other members agreed to move forward with Tom's suggestion.

Guiding Questions

- What were some of the characteristics of institutionalizing cultural knowledge expressed by members of the team?
- Based on this brief conversation, where might you locate the board members on each of the Essential Elements on Table 2.3?
- What evidence would indicate your assessment?
- What future steps might the superintendent's leadership team and the board consider as they plan for additional benchmarking steps on their way to institutionalizing cultural knowledge?

PROFESSIONAL LEARNING FOR GENERAL EDUCATORS

Perhaps one of the best ways to develop professional learning in schools is through professional learning communities. Learning communities provide opportunities for you and colleagues to learn about yourselves and one another in a supportive, professional environment (Nuri-Robins, Lindsey, Lindsey, & Terrell, 2012). As stated earlier and often, we believe the growth and sustainability of professional learning requires reflection and dialogue on a personal and organizational level. Reflective practice as part of a systems thinking approach viewed through the lens of cultural proficiency engages learning community participants in the following:

- Examining your own personal beliefs and values
- Examining the policies and practices of the school/district
- Examining the culture of your community
- Examining disaggregated data to create an instructional plan focused on improving achievement of all demographic groups of students (Lindsey, Jungwirth, Pahl, & Lindsey, 2009)

These activities occurring in a learning community context will enhance the possibility of institutionalizing culturally proficient practices that meet the needs of all students, intentionally the linguistically and culturally diverse students. One example of a professional learning strategy to enhance shared understanding of a change initiative is a whole-group or community book study. A means for achieving deepening personal and schoolwide efficacy is to engage in a book study using this book. The dialogic activity in the Going Deeper section that follows offers a professional learning strategy aligned with the Essential Element presented in the Westfield Case Story.

GOING DEEPER

This chapter presented the Essential Element of institutionalizing cultural knowledge. We offered a final Westfield School District case story as an example of one school district providing leadership toward culturally proficient practices focused on adapting to the changing demographics of the school and surrounding community. How LGBT students are valued and taught can no longer be left to chance. The chapter offered a vignette and guiding questions to assist educators and school teams in institutionalizing policies and practices for working with their LGBT students and their communities. You were provided numerous critical, reflective, and mediational questions to guide your thinking about your own practice and interactions with your colleagues. And we shared one example of a professional learning strategy (a whole-group or community book study) designed to help you, your colleagues, and the community in which you institutionalize the cultural knowledge you have gained about the rich diversity within your school community.

As you think about the information and reflective activities in this chapter, take a few minutes to respond to the following questions:

- What are some key learnings that are emerging for you?
- What assumptions about your students were you holding?

- In what ways have these assumptions guided your teaching behaviors?
- What assumptions do you hold about LGBT students? Straight students?
- In what ways have these assumptions guided your decisions about curriculum, instruction, and assessment?

Personal Reflection: Now that you know what you know and, you have surfaced and examined your assumptions, about institutionalizing cultural knowledge, what are you willing to do? What might it take to create a school and community culture in support of LGBT students, colleagues, and communities?

_____

_____

_____

_____

Dialogic Activity: With a group of your colleagues, engage in a dialogue to reach shared understanding of *a professional development program in support of LGBT students, colleagues, and community members.* Continue the dialogue throughout small learning communities in the school district. Once shared understanding has been reached, what might be some resources, strategies, and structures that could be developed and activated to support all learners, with emphasis on LGBT students?

Part III is the concluding section of this book. Chapter 11 presents you with a call to action! As we have asked you before, now that you know what you know, what are you willing to do?

Part III

Next Steps

Now that you know what you know, what are you willing to do?

11

Moving From Bystander to Ally

We ought to be providing environments that enable each youngster in our schools to find a place in the educational sun.

—Elliot Eisner (2001, p. 372)

Social justice initiatives by their very nature imply action. A person cannot be a bystander and be engaged in socially just initiatives. Whether you are a person relatively new to the notion of lesbian, gay, bisexual, and transgender (LGBT) people being "targets" of systemic oppression or a heterosexual person aspiring to be an ally to LGBT communities or a LGBT person who is an ally to groups within the LGBT community, being an ally means taking action on your part. Before getting too involved with what it takes to be viewed as an ally, let's first discuss what being an ally means. Evans and Washington (2010) note that "defining yourself as an ally is somewhat presumptuous" (p. 419). They also caution that being an ally is not an act of self-declaration; rather, allies are best determined by members of the LGBT communities.

The "inside-out" process of change is fundamental to being an ally and involves having a strong sense of your own heterosexual culture as emphasized in Chapter 6 in this book. We also emphasized in Chapter 2 that understanding the systemic oppression of heterosexism but failing to engage in examinations of cultural privilege will negate even the best of intentions and result in your being experienced as inauthentic.

AUTHORS' NOTE: For purposes of consistency, material in this chapter is adapted from an earlier Cultural Proficiency work. Randall B. Lindsey, Michelle S. Karns, & Keith Myatt, *Culturally Proficient Education: An Asset-Based Response to Conditions of Poverty*, Thousand Oaks, CA: Corwin, 2010.

BEING AN ALLY: THE INSIDE-OUT PROCESS BEGINS WITH YOU

This chapter is designed for you to develop a personal plan for yourself using Cultural Proficiency as a lens to guide your work. Throughout this book, you have had the opportunity

- to reflect on your inside-out process for learning about your own culture, the culture of your school, and the culture of the community you serve;
- to reflect on your thinking and your practice; and
- to read and study, either alone or with colleagues, case story vignettes from the Westfield Unified School District.

In this chapter, you are encouraged to summarize your learning and to design how you want to function as a culturally proficient educator committed to access and equity for the LGBT colleagues and students in your school as well as for parents and community members. Evans and Washington (2010) describe four levels of ally involvement that closely align with the Tools of Cultural Proficiency:

- *Awareness* is the first level. It is important to become more aware of who you are and how you are different from and similar to LGBT people. Such awareness can be gained through conversations with LGBT individuals, attending awareness-building workshops, reading about LGBT life, and self-examination.

- *Knowledge/education* is the second level. You must begin to acquire knowledge about sexual and gender identities and the experiences of LGBT people. This step includes learning about laws, policies, and practices and how they affect LGBT people, in addition to educating yourself about LGBT culture and the norms of this community. Contacting local and national LGBT organizations for information can be very helpful.

- *Skills* make up the third level. This area is the one in which people often fall short because of fear or lack of resources or supports. You must develop skills in communicating the knowledge that you have learned. These skills can be acquired by attending workshops, role-playing certain situations with friends, developing support connections, or practicing interventions or awareness raising in safe settings.

- *Action* is the last, but most important, level and is the most frightening step. There are many challenges and liabilities for heterosexuals in taking actions to end oppression of LGBT people. . . . Nonetheless, action is, without doubt, the only way we can effect change in the society as a whole; for if we keep our awareness, knowledge, and skill to ourselves we deprive the rest of the world of what we have learned, thus keeping them from having the fullest possible life. (p. 418)

AN INVITATION

Our invitation for you is to use this chapter to organize your thinking. Return to the reflective and dialogic thinking you recorded in previous chapters. Take time to organize your thinking in terms of basic learning and continuous improvement for yourself and for your school or school system in service to LGBT communities.

Personal and Organizational Change

We introduced Dilts's model for personal and organizational change in Chapter 2, Table 2.4, by noting its alignment with Cultural Proficiency's inside-out approach to change (Dilts, 1994; Garmston & Wellman, 1999). You may recall the premise of Dilts's nested levels is the change that occurs at one level affects each subsequent level. The two lowest "nests" of Dilts's model, "behaviors" and "environment," is where change often begins for schools. This is most often the case with change that is externally imposed such as with No Child Left Behind or other compliance-driven change.

Our experience is that compliance-driven diversity and equity-related changes are too often limited to specific mandates that are important but that render LGBT communities invisible. Inclusive leadership seizes equity-related opportunities through assuming the moral responsibility to provide for the educational needs of all students as well as provide for an inclusive environment for fellow colleagues, parents, and community members. Dilts's model and the Tools of Cultural Proficiency provide a template and means to chart the continuous improvements in your own educational practice as well as that of your school or school system. In this chapter, you are invited to reflect and summarize your thinking. This reflection process may be your personal journey and/or it may be a dialogic journey taken with colleagues.

Your Personal Journey With LGBT Communities

You have the opportunity to bring forward your work from earlier chapters and summarize your learning. For purposes of planning, we ask you to consider your learning in two domains—your own personal journey and your journey as an educator working with students and parents/guardians serving LGBT communities.

Your Personal Journey. Take a few moments and consider the following questions as invitations to think deeply. Space is provided to record your responses:

Describe what you have learned, or affirmed, about your attitudes toward people from LGBT communities.

_____

_____

_____

_____

What support factors exist for you in service to LGBT students? In service to LGBT colleagues? In service to LGBT parents/community members?

_____

_____

_____

_____

Describe ways in which the case story members in this book resonated in your personal or professional lives.

_____

_____

_____

_____

How might you now facilitate discussions about LGBT issues among close friends, coworkers, community members, and students?

_____

_____

_____

_____

How might you now support LGBT students, their families, and their friends?

_____

_____

_____

_____

In what ways do the tools of Cultural Proficiency provide insight for you as a person living in a diverse society that values people's sexual orientation and gender diversity?

_____

_____

_____

_____

Your Professional Journey. In this section, you have the opportunity to examine your role as an educator and a member of a school and school system.

What might be some ways educators limit their effectiveness when working with students and parents/guardians from LGBT communities?

_____

_____

_____

_____

What might be some ways schools as organizations limit their effectiveness in service to LGBT communities?

_____

_____

_____

_____

What can you do to overcome these limitations?

_____

_____

_____

_____

Think about your role as an educator (teacher, leader, and/or policy maker) and describe *your areas of confidence* about educating *LGBT students.*

_____

_____

_____

_____

Think about your role as an educator (teacher, leader, and/or policy maker) and describe *your areas of confidence* about meeting the needs of *LGBT colleagues.*

_____

_____

_____

_____

Think about your role as an educator (teacher, leader, and/or policy maker) and describe *your areas of confidence* about meeting the needs of *LGBT parents/community members.*

_____

_____

_____

_____

Continue thinking about your role as an educator (teacher, leader, and/or policy maker) and describe *what you need to learn* about serving the educational needs of people from LGBT communities.

_____

_____

_____

_____

Commitments

The usefulness of this book may be measured by your commitments. To this point, your personal learning has been guided by your reflective responses to questions throughout this book and by your own and your colleagues' dialogic responses. The following questions can be used for either personal or professional planning or in community with colleagues.

What do you want for your students from LGBT communities that is within your areas of influence?

_____

_____

_____

_____

What are you willing to commit to doing over the next three years to realize the goal(s) you have set *in service to your students* from LGBT communities?

_____

_____

_____

_____

What are you willing to commit to doing over the next year to realize the goal(s) you have set *in service to LGBT students, colleagues, and parents/ community members?*

_____

_____

_____

_____

What are you willing to commit to over the next week (yes, seven days!) to realize the goal(s) you have set *in service to LGBT communities?*

_____

_____

_____

_____

CONVERSATIONS MATTER

Initially you picked this book and have continued reading it because you care about the education of all students, in particular for the people who are the focus of this book—students and their families, colleagues, or employees who are gay, lesbian, bisexual, or transgender and those who are allies of the LGBT communities. You have continued reading and responding to the prompts throughout this book because you want to improve your craft. Most likely, you believe that our democracies have the capacity to be inclusive of people from all sexual orientation and gender identity groups. You want to be part of a group that solves problems. As Margaret Wheatley (2002) says, "Be brave enough to start a conversation that matters"(p. 145).

Why We Do This Work

RANDALL LINDSEY

Why I Do This Work

In the efforts to find and locate support for social justice in our society, sexual orientation issues may be the levers for the deepest applications of equity in the modern era. The disparities created and nurtured around issues of race—African American and Native First Nations, for example—were readily apparent to me in my early years as an educator. However, it took me a while longer to recognize that my passion around issues of race was deeply influenced by the inequities I observed and sometimes felt around social class. Once I began to understand racism and the link to privilege and entitlement, then issues of gender and sexism were straightforward. They were just plain wrong.

Issues of sexual orientation have not been easy for me to wrestle with, both because of my own embedded assumptions and because of the systemic discrimination that I learned to see—heterosexism. One of the things I have learned about myself in this pursuit of reducing and eliminating heterosexism is the power of internalized homophobia. I recognize that my own homophobia stems from quasi-religious roots. I use the term *quasi* to separate "church" from religion. For me, I have seen how church has been used (in the Christian world, at least) to define and deepen the "isms." Nowhere have these teachings been used more powerfully than on issues of sexual orientation.

A challenge for me has been the intractability of race and the reality that sexual orientation can be hidden. Even though there should be no need to hide sexual orientation, the choice is always present, in contrast to one's race being observable. However, in the Western world, we have a history of hostile reaction to both. I often wonder about issues of race within LGBT communities. Regardless of my "wondering," there is the reality that I can opt out of confronting inequities with either race or sexuality, which is what I see in too many schools. Being an ally and an advocate must lead to action—and that is why I do this work.

My lesson from doing the work of social justice has been the reality that society actually agrees on whom to marginalize. I can see no defense for people engaged in education having the power or authority to decide whom they want to educate based on the cultural identities of the students. Yet I know that happens. Therefore, I want to be part of a legacy of leaving this society better than when I entered it and profited from it.

RICHARD DIAZ

Why I Do This Work

As a gay Latino man, I remember my struggle in high school wondering why I had the sexual feelings that I had. There was really no one to talk to, and I was scared to mention this to anyone. I was in a Catholic high school that, although very progressive about civil rights, did not talk about the "homosexual" issues.

I remember in college having a crush on a fellow student but being afraid to talk to him about it. We had lunch together, we studied together, and we talked about his child and ex-wife. He talked about how he had been in the army for two years. So I thought he was straight. Imagine my surprise five years later to run into him at a gay bar. He died of AIDS a year later.

I remember going to my first gay bar, one that a stranger on the street recommended. I was shocked to see so many Latinos in the bar, but then I was relieved that I was not alone. I no longer felt like the lone gay Latino in the world.

Why do I do this work? I do not want children to be afraid to talk about their feelings. I want teachers to be able to speak with their students and students to feel safe to talk to their teachers. I want children to be able to share with their parents and parents to be able to listen.

I do this work because I want gay men and women to know that it is OK to tell someone they care about them and that they have the right to love someone of the same sex. I do this work to take the fear out of gay and so that all people recognize us as equal citizens of the planet.

I do this work because I want to create a better and more compassionate society.

I do this work because I care.

KIKANZA NURI-ROBINS

Why I Do This Work

- When I was in elementary school, I remember hearing my step-father say to my mother that he was afraid my brother was going to be a sissy.
- The family went swimming at a public pool when I was very young. I had never seen an adult woman naked, and my mother hastily dragged me out of the dressing room. We were the last to get in the car. "What took you so long?" my father asked. "She was staring at the women getting dressed," my mother said to embarrass me. I was, but I didn't know why I was embarrassed.
- One Halloween, one of the neighbor boys, who was in high school, dressed up as a woman. He put oranges in a bra and his sister did his makeup. No one recognized him. When my mother realized who it was, she voiced her disapproval loudly. It was OK for a boy to dress as a girl for Halloween, as long as he still looked like a boy and didn't seem to enjoy it as much as our neighbor did.
- In college, while I was living in a commune, gay men were described hatefully as "punks."
- Any women who appeared to enjoy one another's company "too much" were accused of "biting on each other."
- My mother used to speak of "confirmed bachelors."
- My girlfriend's mother called me a girly girl, with some surprise.
- After I left my husband, he told me that he used to wish that I was gay so that if he left me, no one would say it was his fault.

I remember wondering about all these things, asking questions and never being given a direct answer. When I finally came to understand the issue, I still didn't get it. All I knew was that being a lesbian was worse than being black or fat or just a woman. So I began to read and kept asking questions and finally found a community that would talk with me. I began to understand the subtext of these comments and conversations I have heard throughout my life. I understood, but I still didn't get it. Then I learned about the continuum of sexual orientation, and I began to understand.

I was told of a child recently—an eight-year-old black, transgender girl (a person who appears to be male, but experiences herself as female and identifies as such)—who is the foster child of two white gay men. She is currently in public school; wears her hair long and dresses in female clothes. The whole family is in therapy, and the parents are working with the school to help them be supportive of their child. They are arming themselves emotionally and legally to get the child safely through middle school. We cannot even think about high school at this date. I am hoping that it is less of an issue then.

When I saw how vociferously my friend Randy advocates for justice for people of color, I thought, I can do that. I speak up for gay men and lesbians because I can; it does not put me in jeopardy, and I can give voice to a voiceless segment of many communities. To paraphrase Hillel the Elder, the leader of the Jewish Supreme Court in the Land of Israel in the early part of the first century CE, "If not now, when? If not me, who?" A corollary to that for me is, if there is room for discrimination against any people, then there is room for discrimination against me. If I am for justice, it is for all people, not just the ones I choose. I do this work, around these issues because I can. I do it because it is the right thing to do. I do it because it could just as well be me as one of my friends.

RAYMOND TERRELL

Why I Do This Work

I have been working as a diversity/social justice advocate for 45 years. As an African American male, my first focus was to address issues of racism. Although I have been able to see some progress made in this arena, I know there is a great deal more to do. Facing resistance by many people to deal with issues of race, I have consistently found communities of educators, corporate folks, and community members who are equally committed to racial justice.

In a discussion with a friend who has worked collaboratively with me on many issues of social justice over the years, the issue of same-sex marriage came up. I assumed that because we share compatible views on discrimination against race, gender, language, age, and exceptionalities that we would hold the same view of social justice for persons who are members of LGBT communities. My assumption was wrong. He did not feel the same way I thought he would about LGBT people. As our discussion continued I began to wonder how many other folks with whom I worked held similar negative attitudes? How many people failed to see that targeting any group of people is the slippery slope that leads to discrimination of any other groups of persons. That conversation caused me to reflect on Freire's concept that "the oppressed, instead of striving for liberation, tend themselves to become oppressors."

I then began to poll the teachers and other educators I worked with about how they approached dealing with social justice and LGBT communities. The responses I received ranged from not dealing with it at all, which makes these persons invisible, to taking a hard stance against seeing the issue as one of social justice. The midposition that some held was an attempt to couch approaching the topic in some politically correct fashion that was tantamount to "kinda being for diversity."

What became clear to me was most folks had very little knowledge, interaction, or experience relating to anyone from LGBT communities. They had never even bothered to seriously look in their own families to determine if there were members of the LGBT community. And even if they had, they had not figured out how to internally or externally address the reality in an open and confirming fashion.

These sets of awareness became major motivation for me to contribute to this book.

DELORES LINDSEY

Why I Do This Work

As a major part of my professional and personal journey, I've been working on who I am as a southern, white, Christian, woman. I was raised in a loving, Christian environment by hard-working parents who believed that education was one of the keys to success. My sisters and my brother were taught to love and care for those who need help and to treat people fairly. These family values guided me well through my years as a child, teen, and young teacher in Mississippi and Louisiana. Growing up in the Deep South is something of which I am both proud and conflicted. I feel a sense of pride when our southern hospitality is acknowledged, and I blush a bit when I'm referred to as a steel magnolia or a southern belle. My heart is heavy, however, when our history of slavery, discrimination, prejudice, and voter oppression are mentioned. When I moved to California in the mid-1980s, I found many of the same issues of racism and prejudice I thought had been isolated and assigned to the South. So, I've spent my 40 plus years as an educator focusing on equity and social justice for all students in classrooms, schools, districts, and universities with which I have been affiliated. I've always looked out for the students that no one else seemed to notice or care about. As a school and program administrator, I made certain that rules, regulations, procedures, and practices were in place to protect students and employees who were targets of injustice and inequity.

When I was a middle-grades administrator in southern California, I began to notice that the students who most often became targets of harassment and bullying were students who "looked or acted gay." Name-calling by the perpetrators was the initial weapon of choice, followed by humiliation through practical jokes, ostracizing behaviors, and finally, outright physical injury. Often, when I confronted the students involved in initiating the bullying behaviors, their responses were, "Aw, we were just kidding. We didn't mean any harm." When I confronted the parents of these students, their responses were usually, "Oh, they weren't meaning any harm. They were just boys being boys . . . playing . . . you know having fun with each other." Or "The girls were just being dramatic, you know, drama teens. They didn't mean to hurt anyone's feelings."

I come to this work for the students who feel isolated, lonely, bullied, and unsafe. I write this book on behalf of those students who committed suicide because the bullies continued to harass them through social media sites or at school in the locker room or in their classrooms and hallways at school. Our LGBT students are the most vulnerable and at risk of being injured because of who they are or want to be. My hope is that this book will help create culturally proficient safe schools and communities for LGBT students and adults to be accepted and valued for who they are.

So how does this book inform my thinking about who I am? I'm still growing as an emerging culturally proficient educator and valuing my southern, Christian roots at the same time. I find no reason for these two worldviews to be in conflict with each other, as I once thought they might. Cultural Proficiency is grounded in the moral imperative of intentionally doing the right things so that all students will grow and learn at levels higher than ever before within safe, educational environments. All students and their families deserve nothing less from all educators.

Resources

Resource A.1: Book Study Guide

A Culturally Proficient Response to LGBT Communities: A Guide for Educators

Randall B. Lindsey, Richard M. Diaz, Kikanza J. Nuri-Robins, Raymond D. Terrell, and Delores B. Lindsey

Corwin 2013

PART I. INTRODUCTION: BACKGROUND, CHALLENGES, AND OPPORTUNITY

Chapter 1: Setting the Context

Content Questions to Consider

- In what ways do you consider sexual orientation and gender identity as equity issues?
- What terminology was new to you? In what ways are you now better informed?
- What do you understand the purpose of this book to be?

Personal Reaction Questions to Consider

- What is your reaction to the intent of this book?
- What are self-assessments about your cultural knowledge of who you are in relation to LGBT individuals and groups?
- What is your reaction to examining and discussing sexual orientation and gender diversity in your school?

Chapter 2: The Tools of Cultural Proficiency

Content Questions to Consider

- Name the Tools of Cultural Proficiency.
- In what ways do you describe the inside-out process?
- How do reflection and dialogue support the inside-out process?
- Describe how and why culture is embraced as an asset to support Cultural Proficiency.
- In what ways are the Guiding Principles as core values consistent with how you view yourself and your school?
- Explain how the Guiding Principles serve to counter the Barriers to Cultural Proficiency.
- In what ways will the Essential Elements provide you with "action" steps on your journey toward Cultural Proficiency?

Personal Reaction Questions to Consider

- What is your reaction to the Barriers Section? To the Guiding Principles as core values?
  - Describe the manner in which the Essential Elements are informed and supported by the Guiding Principles.
  - In what ways do the Essential Elements serve as standards for personal, professional behavior?
- What is your reaction, personally or professionally, as you become acquainted with the Tools?
- What more do you want to know/learn about Cultural Proficiency?

Chapter 3: Equality and Equity Are Both Important, Just Not the Same

Content Questions to Consider
- What do you understand *equality* and *equity* to be? In what ways are they similar? Different?
- What new insights might you have from the historical consideration of the terms *equality* and *equity*?
- How does one move from recognizing barriers to engaging in proactive action?

Personal Reaction Questions to Consider

- What are your reactions or feelings about the description and discussion of equity and equality?

- How do you describe personal responsibility for addressing issues related to oppression experienced by LGBT communities? In what ways are you involved?

Chapter 4: Understanding Our History Helps Shape Our Future

Content Questions to Consider

- What new insights to our history might you have?
- In what ways do you describe North American exceptionalism?
- Describe "heteronormative worldview."

Personal Reaction Questions to Consider

- In what ways does this chapter contribute to your knowledge of your values and assumptions about people whose sexual orientation or gender identity might be different from yours?
- This chapter frames sexual orientation and gender identity as human rights issues in modern society. What is your reaction to this perspective?

PART II. WESTFIELD UNIFIED SCHOOL DISTRICT

Chapter 5: Creating Safe Space: Moving From Compliance to Advocacy

Content Questions to Consider

- In what ways do you describe moving from compliance to advocacy?
- How might you describe bullying as an issue in our schools?
- Describe key components in the two-phase approach to bullying.
- How do the authors describe "safe space"? What examples do you have of safe spaces at your school?

Personal Reaction Questions to Consider

- What reactions do you have to the information about the extent of bullying and its harmful effects?
- What information and data do you have about your own school? How do you react to the prospect of having such information about your school?
- What are two or three goals you might want to set for learning about LGBT communities in your school?

Chapter 6: Assessing Cultural Knowledge

Content Questions to Consider

- In what ways do the Essential Elements serve as standards for organizational policy and practice?
- How might the Essential Elements be useful for you and your school?
- How might you describe the Essential Element, assessing cultural knowledge?
- In what ways does Superintendent Charlton describe assessing cultural knowledge?

Personal Reaction Questions to Consider

- In what ways is Cultural Proficiency a *journey*?
- How do you describe your understanding of assessing cultural knowledge?
- In what ways can you and your school use the information from this chapter?

Chapter 7: Valuing Diversity

Content Questions to Consider

- How might you describe the Essential Element, valuing diversity?
- In what ways do you describe the four components of diversity?
- What is the valuing diversity issue in the case story? Who needs help and why do you think it to be so?

Personal Reaction Question to Consider

- What were your thoughts and personal reactions about the information in this chapter? In what ways do your reactions inform your future communications choices?
- In what ways might you and your school use the information from this chapter?

Chapter 8: Managing the Dynamics of Difference

Content Questions to Consider

- How might you describe the Essential Element, managing the dynamics of diversity?
- What is the dynamics of diversity issue in the case story? Who needs help and why do you think it to be so?

Personal Reaction Questions to Consider

- What were your thoughts and personal reactions about the information in this chapter? In what ways do your reactions inform your future choices for working in your school?
- In what ways can you and your school use the information from this chapter?

Chapter 9: Adapting to Diversity

Content Questions to Consider

- Please describe the Essential Element, adapting to diversity.
- What is the adapting to diversity issue in the case story? Who needs help and why do you think it to be so?
- What does it mean to be an "ally"?

Personal Reaction Questions to Consider

- What were your thoughts and personal reactions about the information in this chapter? In what ways do your reactions inform your future choices for you and your school?
- In what ways can you and your school use the information from this chapter?

Chapter 10: Institutionalizing Cultural Knowledge: You, Your School, and Your Community

Content Questions to Consider

- How do you describe the Essential Element, institutionalizing cultural knowledge?
- You have been reading the phrase "inside-out" process throughout this book. What does it mean to you now? What has been added to your knowledge? In what ways does it apply to schools?
- In the context of this chapter, in what ways do you describe *transformation?*
- What is the issue in the case story? Who needs help and why do you think it to be so?

Personal Reaction Questions to Consider

- What were your thoughts and personal reactions about the information in this chapter? In what ways do your reactions inform your future choices for you and your school?

- In what ways can you and your school use the information from this chapter?

PART III. NEXT STEPS

Chapter 11: Moving From Bystander to Ally

Content Questions to Consider

- What are the four levels for becoming an ally? In what ways do the four levels align with the Essential Elements?
- Why do conversations matter?

Personal Reaction Questions to Consider

- What are your reactions in responding to the progression of prompts in this chapter?
- In what ways can you and your school use the information from this chapter?
- Now that you know what you know, what are you willing to do?

Resource A.2:
The "Apps" of Cultural Proficiency

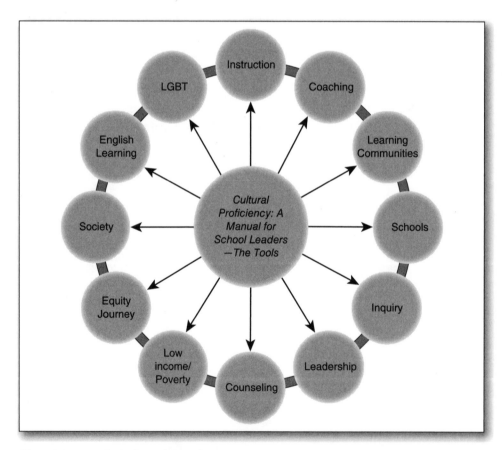

The "Apps of Cultural Proficiency" is a pictorial representation of the Cultural Proficiency books. The original and core book, *Cultural Proficiency: A Manual for School Leaders*, now in third edition, presents our most detailed description of the Tools of Cultural Proficiency. The books radiating from the Manual also present the basic Tools in an applied manner relating to the books' intent (e.g., instruction, coaching, etc.).

Resource B: Quick Glossary of Terms

This is a list of commonly used terms in conversations by and about LGBT communities. It is not an exhaustive list; it includes words to support your continued learning.

Coming out	The process of letting someone know that you are not a heterosexual.
Gay	The preferred term for homosexual males.
Gender	The identification one has as a male or female. Gender is an internal expression; it cannot be assigned to a person by others.
Heterosexism	The belief that heterosexuals and heterosexual relationships are superior to homosexual interactions and the power to impose sanctions against homosexuals.
Homophobia	The fear of homosexuality.
Homosexual	Males and females who are emotionally and sexually attracted to the same gender.
Lesbian	The preferred term for homosexual females.
LGBT	Lesbian, gay, bisexual, and transgender.
Sexual identity	How one sees oneself physically as male or female or neither.
Sexual orientation	How one is drawn to physical relationships with one's same gender or another is one's orientation.
Sexual preference	A term that implies that sexual attraction and gender identification is a choice rather than a biological fact.
Transgender	Males or females who appear to be one gender physiologically but who identify as the other gender or neither gender; this may vary during one's life. A male who feels like a female inside is a transgender female.

Resource C.1: Sexual Orientation Questionnaire

Chapter 8 Activity 1

(Please respond candidly. You will <u>not</u> be asked to submit this questionnaire.)

1. What do you think caused your heterosexuality?

2. When and how did you first decide you were a heterosexual?

3. Is it possible your heterosexuality is just a phase you may grow out of?

4. Is it possible your heterosexuality stems from a neurotic fear of others of the same sex?

5. Isn't it possible that all you need is a good gay lover?

6. Heterosexuals have histories of failures in gay relationships. Do you think you may have turned to heterosexuality out of fear of rejection?

7. If you've never slept with a person of the same sex, how do you know you wouldn't prefer that?

8. If heterosexuality is normal, why are a disproportionate number of mental patients heterosexual?

9. Your heterosexuality doesn't offend me as long as you don't try to force it on me. To whom have you disclosed your heterosexual tendencies? How did they react?

10. Why do you people feel compelled to seduce others into your sexual orientation?

11. If you choose to parent children, would you want them to be heterosexual knowing the problems they would face?

12. The great majority of child molesters are heterosexuals. Do you really consider it safe to expose your children to heterosexual teachers?

13. Why do you insist on being so obvious and making a public spectacle of your heterosexuality? Can't you just be what you are and keep it quiet?

14. How can you ever hope to become a whole person if you limit yourself to a compulsive, exclusive heterosexual object choice and remain unwilling to explore and develop your normal, natural, healthy, God-given homosexual potential?

15. Heterosexuals are noted for assigning themselves and each other to narrowly restricted, stereotyped sex roles. Why do you cling to such unhealthy role-playing?

16. How can you enjoy a fully satisfying sexual experience or deep emotional connection with a person of the opposite sex when the obvious physical, biological, and temperamental differences between you are so vast?

17. How can a man understand what pleases a woman sexually or vice versa?

18. Why do heterosexuals place so much emphasis on sex?

19. With all the societal support marriage receives, the divorce rate is spiraling. Fifty percent of first marriages fail. The rate for second marriages is higher. Why are there so few stable relationships among heterosexuals?

20. Considering the menace of overpopulation, how could the human race survive if everyone were heterosexual like you?

21. There seem to be very few happy heterosexuals. Techniques have been developed with which you might be able to change if you really want to change. Have you considered trying aversion therapy?

22. A disproportionate number of criminals, welfare recipients, and other irresponsible or antisocial types are heterosexual. Why would anyone want to hire a heterosexual for a responsible position?

23. Do heterosexuals hate and/or distrust others of their own sex? Is that what makes them heterosexual?

24. Why are heterosexuals so promiscuous?

25. Why do you make a point of attributing heterosexuality to famous people? Is it to justify your own heterosexuality?

From Steve Berman and Martin Rochlin: "A Reversal of Questions Frequently Asked of Lesbians and Gay Men," January 1977.

Revised by Griff Humphreys, May 1981. (These people were staff members of the University of California, San Diego, campus community and attended professional development facilitated by the authors.) Class handout, available at http://www.pflagwestchester.org/PrideWorks/ 2008_Handouts/HeterosexualQuestionnaire.pdf/

Resource C.2: Unpacking the Knapsack of Sexual Orientation Privilege

Chapter 8 Activity 2

1 = never, 2 = rarely, 3 = sometimes, 4 = often, 5 = always					
1. I can legally marry any adult of my choice in the state in which I reside.	1	2	3	4	5
2. I can legally marry any adult of my choice in any state in my country.	1	2	3	4	5
3. I can marry any adult of my choice and know that my marriage will be recognized by my faith community.	1	2	3	4	5
4. I can be sure that if I need legal or medical help, my sexual orientation will not be an impediment to good and appropriate service.	1	2	3	4	5
5. My spouse or significant other and I can hold hands while walking down most streets together without concern for our safety.	1	2	3	4	5
6. I can, if I wish, put my spouse or partner's photograph on my office desk without fear of negative reaction from coworkers.	1	2	3	4	5
7. I am never asked to speak for all people of my sexual orientation.	1	2	3	4	5
8. My partner and I can choose from a wide array of vacation and hotel accommodations without fearing mistreatment due to perceptions of our sexual orientation.	1	2	3	4	5

(Continued)

(Continued)

9. I can be reasonably sure that my child will not be harassed because of my sexual orientation.	1	2	3	4	5
10. I can be reasonably sure that my children's teachers and educational institutions will recognize and fairly represent my sexual orientation in the curriculum.	1	2	3	4	5
11. I can send my gay child to school knowing my child will not be subjected to discrimination from the teachers and administrators.	1	2	3	4	5
12. I have never felt a need to hide my sexual orientation from family members.	1	2	3	4	5
13. I have never felt a need to hide my sexual orientation from classmates or coworkers.	1	2	3	4	5
14. I can assume that others' knowledge of my sexual orientation will not adversely affect me in my business or professional life.	1	2	3	4	5
15. I can turn on the television or open the front page of the paper and see people of my sexual orientation widely represented.	1	2	3	4	5

Adapted by Mary Galloway from McIntosh (1988).

Resource D: Community Resources

Justice and Equity for LGBT Communities

Resource	Description of Services/Site	Link
ACT for Youth Center	ACT (Assets Coming Together) for Youth Center of Excellence connects research to practice in the areas of positive youth development and adolescent sexual health.	http://www.actforyouth .net/
Advocates for Youth	Established in 1980 as the Center for Population Options, Advocates for Youth champions efforts that help young people make informed and responsible decisions about their reproductive and sexual health. Advocates believes it can best serve the field by boldly advocating for a more positive and realistic approach to adolescent sexual health. Advocates focuses its work on young people ages 14 to 25 in the United States and around the globe.	Creating Safe Space for GLBTQ Youth: A Toolkit http://www .advocatesforyouth.org
American Library Association: Rainbow Books Bibliography	The Rainbow Project was created as a grassroots effort in 2007 to provide young people with books that reflect GLBTQ individuals, groups, and experiences. Although many more books with GLBTQ content are available to this audience than in the past, many of these are not identified as	http://www.ala.org/ glbtrt/rainbow/ bibliographies

(Continued)

(Continued)

Resource	Description of Services/Site	Link
	such, necessitating such a bibliography. The Rainbow Project was originally a Social Responsibilities Round Table (SRRT) task force but became affiliated also with Gay, Lesbian, Bisexual, and Transgendered Round Table (GLBTRT) during the American Library Association Midwinter Meeting 2009.	
American Psychological Association: Healthy Lesbian, Gay, and Bisexual Students Project	The Healthy LGB Students Project is funded by the Division of Adolescent and School Health of the Centers for Disease Control and Prevention (CDC-DASH) to provide capacity-building assistance to schools and other organizations that serve gay and bisexual young men at risk for HIV infection, especially African American and Latino youth. Our goal is to help schools, families, and communities promote the healthy growth and full development of lesbian, gay, bisexual, and questioning (LGBQ) youth.	http://www.apa.org/pi/lgbt/programs/hlgbsp/index.aspx
Center for Adaptive Schools	Schools in which faculty members feel a collective responsibility for student learning produce greater learning gains than do schools in which teachers work as isolated practitioners. Teachers in Adaptive Schools are successfully responsive to the changing needs of students, standards and curriculum demands. The work of the Center for Adaptive Schools is informed by research in the new sciences, integrating this work with change models, best educational practices, learning theory, and research on group and adult development.	http://www.adaptiveschools.com
Center for Cognitive Coaching	Cognitive Coaching is a skill set that provides educators long-term investment in creating a culture that values the development of thoughtful teaching and administrative practices, self-directed learning and a support for mediation of thinking. Since human beings operate with a rich variety of cultural, personal, and cognitive style differences, skillful coaching supports these differences as resources for learning. Appreciating and	http://www.cognitivecoaching.com

Resource	Description of Services/Site	Link
	working with style differences requires awareness, knowledge, skills, and positive attitudes for all involved.	
Centers for Disease Control and Prevention	LGBT Youth Resources for youth as well as educators	http://www.cdc.gov/ lgbthealth/youth-resources.htm
Cuéntame	**Mission** A place for Latinos! Whether you are a sports fan, movie fan, activist, artist, student, parent, organizer, Latino or not, award-winning novelist, astronaut, actor, painter, or anything else, all are welcome here! Tell us your story! Focus is not only on LGBT, but you can find some stories about gay and lesbian Latinos.	http://www.facebook .com/cuentame#!/ cuentame
DeColores Queer Orange County	**Mission:** DeColores Queer Orange County creates opportunities for social engagement, community visibility, and political activism by organizing cultural events, support groups, civic actions, and annual conference. The Vision of DeColores Queer Orange County is to create empowering social, supportive, and political spaces for Queer Latin@s in Orange County.	http://decoloresqueeroc .tumblr.com/aboutus
GALE Learning Community	The Alliance for LGBT Education provides information and a platform for exchange for everyone who is concerned with education about the rights of lesbian women, gay men, bisexuals, and transgender people.	http://www.lgbt-education.info/
GLSEN	GLSEN, the Gay, Lesbian & Straight Education Network, is the leading national education organization focused on ensuring safe schools for all students. GLSEN seeks to develop school climates where difference is valued for the positive contribution it makes to creating a more vibrant and diverse community.	http://www.glsen.org/ cgi-bin/iowa/all/home/ index.html

(Continued)

(Continued)

Resource	Description of Services/Site	Link
New Day Films Talking About Gay Issues in School	*It's Elementary* takes cameras into classrooms across the U.S. to look at one of today's most controversial issues—whether and how gay issues should be discussed in schools. It features elementary and middle schools where (mainly heterosexual) teachers are challenging the prevailing political climate and its attempt to censor any dialogue in schools about gay people.	http://www.newday .com/films/Its_ Elementary.html
Parents, Families and Friends of Lesbians and Gays: PFLAG	PFLAG promotes the health and well-being of lesbian, gay, bisexual and transgender persons, their families and friends through support, to cope with an adverse society; education, to enlighten an ill-informed public; and advocacy, to end discrimination and to secure equal civil rights. Parents, Families and Friends of Lesbians and Gays provides opportunity for dialogue about sexual orientation and gender identity and acts to create a society that is healthy and respectful of human diversity.	http://community .pflag.org/Page.aspx? pid=194&srcid=-2
Safe Schools Coalition	The Safe Schools Coalition is an international public-private partnership in support of gay, lesbian, bisexual, and transgender youth. Resources for K–12 Teachers & Curriculum Specialist Classroom Resources (books, curricula, videos, websites and music)	http://www.safeschools coalition.org/RG-teachers_k-12.html
Story of Jorge Gutierrez Who Is Undocumented and Queer	Great video of undocumented queer Latino who is working to get the voices of the queer undocumented Latinos heard.	http://www.huffington post.com/2012/02/14/ undocumented-queer-latino-teens_n_ 1270994.html
The Latino Equality Alliance	The Latino Equality Alliance (LEA) is a broad-based coalition made up of organizations serving LGBT Latino populations, ally organizations, and individuals deeply rooted in both the LGBT and Latino communities.	http://www.latino equalityalliance.com/ About

Resource	Description of Services/Site	Link
	LEA is active in promoting community activism and awareness throughout Los Angeles County.	
The Learning Network: Teaching and Learning With the *New York Times*	A collection of *New York Times* and Learning Network materials that includes lesson plans, Student Opinion questions and other teaching materials, along with *Times* multimedia and feature articles, including historical articles published since 1980.	http://learning.blogs .nytimes.com/2011/11/ 22/teaching-and-learning-about-gay-history-and-issues/
xQsíMagazine	The mission of *xQsí Magazine* is simple. We want to publish an LGBTQ Latin@ multimedia publication that reexamines identity, guides critical dialogue, and inspires political action through content that reflects the diversity and dignity of our community. We believe in our community. We have a vision for our community. We want to live in a world where LGBTQ Latin@s fully express their true voice and are acknowledged, embraced, and celebrated.	http://xqsimagazine .com/
2009 Directory of LGBTQ People of Color Organizations and Projects in the U.S.	This directory addresses autonomous LGBT People of Color Organizations, led by LGBTQ people of color, as well as programs and projects for LGBTQ People of Color housed in broader-themed organizations.	http://www.lgbtfunders .org/files/FLGI_POC_ Dirctry_2009.pdf

Resource E:
Cultural Proficiency Books' Essential Questions

Book	Authors	Focus and Essential Questions
Cultural Proficiency: A Manual for School Leaders, 3rd ed., 2009	Randall B. Lindsey, Kikanza J. Nuri-Robins, Raymond D. Terrell	This book is an introduction to Cultural Proficiency. The book provides readers with extended discussion of each of the Tools and the historical framework for diversity work. • What is Cultural Proficiency? How does Cultural Proficiency differ from other responses to diversity? • In what ways do I incorporate the Tools of Cultural Proficiency into my practice? • How do I use the resources and activities to support professional development? • How do I identify barriers to student learning? • How do the Guiding Principles and Essential Elements support better education for students? • What does the "inside-out" process mean for me as an educator? • How do I foster challenging conversations with colleagues? • How do I extend my own learning?
Culturally Proficient Instruction: A Guide for People Who Teach, 3rd ed., 2012	Kikanza J. Nuri-Robins, Delores B. Lindsey, Randall B. Lindsey, Raymond D. Terrell	This book focuses on the five Essential Elements and can be helpful to anyone in an instructional role. This book can be used as a workbook for a study group. • What does it mean to be a culturally proficient instructor? • How do I incorporate Cultural Proficiency into a school's learning community processes?

Book	Authors	Focus and Essential Questions
		• How do we move from "mind-set" or "mental model" to a set of practices in our school? • How does my "cultural story" support being effective as an educator with my students? • In what ways might we apply the Maple View Story to our learning community? • In what ways can I integrate the Guiding Principles of Cultural Proficiency with my own values about learning and learners? • In what ways do the Essential Elements as standards inform and support our work with the Common Core standards? • How do I foster challenging conversations with colleagues? • How do I extend my own learning?
The Culturally Proficient School: An Implementation Guide for School Leaders, 2005 (2nd edition due 2013).	Randall B. Lindsey, Laraine M. Roberts, Franklin CampbellJones	This book guides readers to examine their schools as cultural organizations and to design and implement approaches to dialogue and inquiry. • In what ways do Cultural Proficiency and school leadership help me close achievement gaps? • What are the communication skills I need to master to support my colleagues when focusing on achievement gap topics? • How do "transactional" and "transformational" changes differ and inform closing achievement gaps in my school/district? • How do I foster challenging conversations with colleagues? • How do I extend my own learning?
Culturally Proficient Coaching: Supporting Educators to Create Equitable Schools, 2007	Delores B. Lindsey, Richard S. Martinez, Randall B. Lindsey	This book aligns the Essential Elements with Costa and Garmston's Cognitive Coaching model. The book provides coaches, teachers, and administrators a personal guidebook with protocols and maps for conducting conversations that shift thinking in support of all students achieving at levels higher than ever before. • What are the coaching skills I need in working with diverse student populations? • In what ways do the Tools of Cultural Proficiency and Cognitive Coaching's States of Mind support my addressing achievement issues in my school? • How do I foster challenging conversations with colleagues? • How do I extend my own learning?

(Continued)

(Continued)

Book	Authors	Focus and Essential Questions
Culturally Proficient Inquiry: A Lens for Identifying and Examining Educational Gaps, 2008	Randall B. Lindsey, Stephanie M. Graham, R. Chris Westphal, Jr., Cynthia L. Jew	This book uses protocols for gathering and analyzing student achievement and access data. Rubrics for gathering and analyzing data about educator practices are also presented. A CD accompanies the book for easy downloading and use of the data protocols. • How do we move from the "will" to educate all children to actually developing our "skills" and doing so? • In what ways do we use the various forms of student achievement data to inform educator practice? • In what ways do we use access data (e.g., suspensions, absences, enrollment in special education or gifted classes) to inform schoolwide practices? • How do we use the four rubrics to inform educator professional development? • How do I foster challenging conversations with colleagues? • How do I extend my own learning?
Culturally Proficient Leadership: The Personal Journey Begins Within, 2009	Raymond D. Terrell, Randall B. Lindsey	This book guides the reader through the development of a cultural autobiography as a means to becoming an increasingly effective leader in our diverse society. The book is an effective tool for use by leadership teams. • How did I develop my attitudes about others' cultures? • When I engage in intentional cross-cultural communication, how can I use those experiences to heighten my effectiveness? • In what ways can I grow into being a culturally proficient leader? • How do I foster challenging conversations with colleagues? • How do I extend my own learning?
Culturally Proficient Learning Communities: Confronting Inequities Through Collaborative Curiosity, 2009	Delores B. Lindsey, Linda D. Jungwirth Jarvis V. N. C. Pahl, Randall B. Lindsey	This book provides readers a lens through which to examine the purpose, the intentions, and the progress of learning communities to which they belong or that they wish to develop. School and district leaders are provided protocols, activities, and rubrics to engage in actions focused on the intersection of race, ethnicity, gender, social class,

Book	Authors	Focus and Essential Questions
		sexual orientation and identity, faith, and ableness with the disparities in student achievement. • What is necessary for a learning community to become a "culturally proficient learning community"? • What is organizational culture and how do I describe my school's culture in support of equity and access? • What are "curiosity" and "collaborative curiosity" and how do I foster them at my school/district? • How will "breakthrough questions" enhance my work as a learning community member and leader? • How do I foster challenging conversations with colleagues? • How do I extend my own learning?
The Cultural Proficiency Journey: Moving Beyond Ethical Barriers Toward Profound School Change, 2010	Franklin CampbellJones, Brenda CampbellJones, Randall B. Lindsey	This book explores cultural proficiency as an ethical construct. It makes transparent the connection between observable behavior and values, assumptions, and beliefs, making change possible and sustainable. The book is appropriate for book study teams. • In what ways does "moral consciousness" inform and support my role as an educator? • How do a school's "core values" become reflected in assumptions held about students? • What steps do I take to ensure that my school and I understand any low expectations we might have? • How do we recognize that our low expectations serve as ethical barriers? • How do I foster challenging conversations with colleagues? • How do I extend my own learning?
Culturally Proficient Education: An Asset-Based Response to Conditions of Poverty, 2010	Randall B. Lindsey, Michelle S. Karns, Keith Myatt	This book is written for educators to learn how to identify and develop the strengths of students from low-income backgrounds. It is an effective learning community resource to promote reflection and dialogue. • What are "assets" that students bring to school? • How do we operate from an "assets-based" perspective?

(Continued)

Book	Authors	Focus and Essential Questions
		• What are my and my school's expectations about students from low-income and impoverished backgrounds? • How do I foster challenging conversations with colleagues? • How do I extend my own learning?
Culturally Proficient Collaboration: Use and Misuse of School Counselors, 2011	Diana L. Stephens, Randall B. Lindsey	This book uses the lens of Cultural Proficiency to frame the American Association of School Counselor's performance standards and Education Trust's Transforming School Counseling Initiative as means for addressing issues of access and equity in schools in collaborative school leadership teams. • How do counselors fit into achievement-related conversations with administrators and teachers? • What is the "new role" for counselors? • How does this "new role" differ from existing views of school counselors? • What is the role of site administrators in this new role of school counselor? • How do I foster challenging conversations with colleagues? • How do I extend my own learning?
A Culturally Proficient Society Begins in School: Leadership for Equity, 2011	Carmella S. Franco, Maria G. Ott, Darline P. Robles	This book frames the life stories of three superintendents through the lens of Cultural Proficiency. The reader is provided the opportunity to design or modify his or her own leadership-for-equity plan. • In what ways is the role of school superintendent related to equity issues? • Why is this topic important to me as a superintendent or aspiring superintendent? • What are the leadership characteristics of a culturally proficient school superintendent? • How do I foster challenging conversations with colleagues? • How do I extend my own learning?
The Best of Corwin: Equity, 2012	Randall B. Lindsey, Ed.	This edited book provides a range of perspectives of published chapters from prominent authors on topics of equity, access, and diversity. It is designed for use by school study groups. • In what ways do these readings support our professional learning?

Book	Authors	Focus and Essential Questions
		• How might I use these readings to engage others in learning conversations to support all students' learning and all educators educating all students?
Culturally Proficient Practice: Supporting Educators of English Learning Students, **2012**	Reyes L. Quezada, Delores B. Lindsey, Randall B. Lindsey	This book guides readers to apply the five Essential Elements of Cultural Competence to their individual practice and their school's approaches to equity. The book works well for school study groups. • In what ways do I foster support for the education of English learning students? • How can I use action research strategies to inform my practice with English learning students? • In what ways might this book support all educators in our district/school? • How do I foster challenging conversations with colleagues? • How do I extend my own learning?
A Culturally Proficient Response to LGBT Communities: A Guide for Educators, **2013**	Randall B. Lindsey, Richard M. Diaz, Kikanza J. Nuri-Robins, Raymond D. Terrell, Delores B. Lindsey	This book guides the reader to understand sexual orientation in a way that provides for the educational needs of all students. The reader explores values, behaviors, policies, and practices that affect lesbian, gay, bisexual, and transgender students, educators, and parents/guardians. • How do I foster support for LGBT colleagues, students, and parents/guardians? • In what ways does our school show that it values LGBT members? • How can I create a safe environment for all students to learn? • To what extent is my school an environment where it is safe for the adults to be open about their sexual orientation? • How do I reconcile my attitudes toward religion and sexuality with my responsibilities as a PreK–12 educator? • How do I foster challenging conversations with colleagues? • How do I extend my own learning?

References and
Further Readings

Badgett, M. V. Lee. (2012, February). *The impact of extending sexual orientation and gender identify non-discrimination requirements to federal contractors.* Los Angeles, CA: UCLA School of Law, Williams Institute.

Blackburn, Mollie V., Clark, Caroline T., Kenney, Lauren M., & Smith, Jill M. (Eds.). (2010). *Acting out: Combating homophobia through teacher activism.* New York, NY: Teachers College Press.

Bochenek, Michael, & Brown, A. Widney. (2001). *Hatred in the hallways: Violence and discrimination against lesbian, gay, bisexual and transgender students in U.S. schools.* New York, NY: Human Rights Watch.

California Assembly Bill 9. Seth's Law. Retrieved from http://www.leginfo .ca.gov/pub/11-12/bill/asm/ab_0001-0050/ab_9_bill_20111009_chaptered .html

CampbellJones, Franklin, CampbellJones, Brenda, & Lindsey, Randall B. (2010). *The cultural proficiency journey: Moving beyond ethical barriers toward profound school change.* Thousand Oaks, CA: Corwin.

Campos, David. (2005). *Understanding gay and lesbian youth: Lessons for straight school teachers, counselors, and administrators.* Lanham, MD: Rowman & Littlefield Education.

Chittister, Joan. (2010, July 26). Ideas in passing: To be a moral force in the world [Weblog message]. Retrieved from http://www.benetvision.org/Ideas_In_ Passing/07_26_10.html

Corbin, Linda K. (2011). *Surviving high school in a heteronormative culture* (Unpublished doctoral dissertation). University of Redlands, Redlands, CA.

Cross, Terry L. (1989). *Toward a culturally competent system of care.* Washington, DC: Georgetown University Child Development Program, Child and Adolescent Service System Program.

Deal, Terrence A., & Kennedy, Allan A. (1982). *Corporate cultures: The rites and rituals of corporate life.* Reading, MA: Addison Wesley.

DeWitt, Peter M. (2012). *Dignity for all: Safeguarding LGBT students.* Thousand Oaks, CA: Corwin.

Dilts, Robert. (1990). *Changing belief systems with NLP.* Capitola, CA: Meta.

Dilts, Robert. (1994). *Effective presentation skills.* Capitola, CA: Meta.

Dixon, Robin. (2012, June 8). [Obituary for Philip Tobias, 1925–2012]. *Los Angeles Times,* p. AA6.

Eisner, Elliot W. (2001). What does it mean to say a school is doing well? *Phi Delta Kappan, 82*(5), 367–372.

Evans, N. J., & Washington, J. (2010). Becoming an ally: A new examination. In Maurianne Adams, Warren J. Blumenfeld, Carmelita (Rosie) Castañeda, Heather W. Hackman, Madeline Peters, & Ximena Zúñiga (Eds.), *Readings for diversity and social justice* (2nd ed., pp. 413–421). New York, NY: Routledge.

Faith-based tolerance. (2012, February 5). *Los Angeles Times*, p. A23.

Fullan, Michael. (2003). *The moral imperative of school leadership.* Thousand Oaks, CA: Corwin Press.

Garmston, Robert J., & Wellman, Bruce M. (1999). *The adaptive school: A sourcebook for developing collaborative groups.* Norwood, MA: Christopher-Gordon.

Hall, M. (2010). Facilitating visibility of LGBTQ issues in public schools: Teacher resistance and teachable moments. In M. V. Blackburn, C. T. Clark, L. M. Kenney, & J. M. Smith (Eds.), *Acting out! Combating homophobia through teacher activism* (pp. 103–113). New York, NY: Teachers College, Columbia University.

Jeppson, Jandy, with Myers-Walls, Judith A. (2010). *Provider-parent partnerships: Child growth and development.* Lafayette, IN: Purdue University Extension, http://www.extension.purdue.edu/providerparent/Child%20Growth-Development/Main-CGD.htm

Kosciw, Joseph G., Greytak, Emily A., Bartkiewicz, Mark J., Boesen, Madelyn J., & Palmer, Neal A. (2012). *The 2011 National School Climate Survey: The experiences of lesbian, gay, bisexual and transgender youth in our nation's schools.* New York, NY: Gay, Lesbian and Straight Education Network.

Kosciw, Joseph G., Greytak, Emily A., Diaz, Elizabeth M., & Bartkiewicz, Mark J. (2010). *The 2009 National School Climate Survey: The experiences of lesbian, gay, bisexual and transgender youth in our nation's schools.* New York, NY: Gay, Lesbian and Straight Education Network.

Lindsey, Delores B., Jungwirth, Linda D., Pahl, Jarvis V. N. C., & Lindsey, Randall B. (2009). *Culturally proficient learning communities: Confronting inequities through collaborative curiosity.* Thousand Oaks, CA: Corwin.

Lindsey, Delores B., Martinez, Richard S., & Lindsey, Randall B. (2007). *Culturally proficient coaching: Supporting educators to create equitable schools.* Thousand Oaks, CA: Corwin Press.

Lindsey, Randall B., Karns, Michelle S., & Myatt, Keith. (2010). *Culturally proficient education: An asset-based response to conditions of poverty.* Thousand Oaks, CA: Corwin.

Lindsey, Randall B., Nuri-Robins, Kikanza, & Terrell, Raymond D. (1999). *Cultural proficiency: A manual for school leaders.* Thousand Oaks, CA: Corwin.

Lindsey, Randall B., Nuri-Robins, Kikanza, & Terrell, Raymond D. (2005). *Cultural proficiency: A manual for school leaders* (2nd ed.). Thousand Oaks, CA: Corwin.

Lindsey, Randall B., Nuri-Robins, Kikanza, & Terrell, Raymond D. (2009). *Cultural proficiency: A manual for school leaders* (3rd ed.). Thousand Oaks, CA: Corwin.

Lindsey, Randall B., Roberts, Laraine M., & CampbellJones, Franklin. (2005). *The culturally proficient school: An implementation guide for school leaders.* Thousand Oaks, CA: Corwin Press.

McIntosh, Peggy. (1988). *White privilege and male privilege: A personal account of coming to see correspondences through work in women's studies* (Working paper No. 189). Wellesley, MA: Wellesley College.

Miller, Neil. (2006). *Out of the past: Gay and lesbian history from 1869 to the present.* New York, NY: Alyson Books.

Murray, Stephen O. (2000). *Homosexualities.* Chicago, IL: University of Chicago Press.

Nuri-Robins, Kikanza J., Lindsey, Delores B., Lindsey, Randall B., & Terrell, Raymond D. (2012). *Culturally proficient instruction: A guide for people who teach* (3rd ed.). Thousand Oaks, CA: Corwin.

Olewus, Dan. (1993). *Bullying in schools: Facts and interventions.* Bergen, Norway: Research Centre for Health Promotion. Retrieved from http://oud.nigz.nl/upload/presentatieolweus.pdf

Ontario Ministry of Education. (2009). *Realizing the promise of diversity: Ontario's equity and inclusive education strategy.* Ottawa, Ontario, Canada: Ministry of Education. www.edu.gov.on.ca

Petrosino, Anthony, Guckenburg, Sarah, DeVoe, Jill, & Hanson, Thomas L. (2010). *What characteristics of bullying, bullying victims, and schools are associated with increased reporting of bullying to school officials?* San Francisco, CA: WestEd. Available at http://www.wested.org/cs/we/view/rs/1042

Quezada, Reyes L., Lindsey, Delores B., & Lindsey, Randall B. (2012). *Culturally proficient practice: Supporting educators of English learning students.* Thousand Oaks, CA: Corwin.

Robers, Simone, Zhang, Jijun, & Truman, Jennifer. (2010). *Indicators of school crime and safety: 2010* (NCES 2011-002/ NCJ 230812). Washington, DC: National Center for Education Statistics.

Schein, Edgar. (1992). *Organization culture and leadership* (2nd ed.). San Francisco, CA: Jossey-Bass.

Schein, Edgar. (2004). *Organization culture and leadership* (3rd ed.). San Francisco, CA: Jossey-Bass.

Schein, Edgar. (2010). *Organization culture and leadership* (4th ed.). San Francisco, CA: Jossey-Bass.

Senge, Peter M., Cambron-McCabe, Nelda H., Lucas, Timothy, Smith, Bryan, Dutton, Janis, & Kleiner, Art (Eds.). (2012). *Schools that learn: A fifth discipline fieldbook for educators, parents, and everyone who cares about education.* New York, NY: Crown Business.

Shulman, Lee. (2012). The six commonplaces of every profession. *HML Notes* [Weblog]. Port Ludlow, WA: The Horace Mann League. http://www.horacemannleague.blogspot.com/?utm_source=HML+Postings+for+March+25%2C+2013&utm_campaign=hml&utm_medium=email

Sue, Derald Wing. (2010). *Microaggressions in everyday life: Race, gender and sexual orientation.* Hoboken, NJ: John Wiley.

Sullivan, Michael K. (2008). Homophobia, history, and homosexuality: Trends for sexual minorities. *Journal of Human Behavior in the Social Environment, 8*(2/3), 247–260. doi:10.1300/J137v08n02_01

Terrell, Raymond D., & Lindsey, Randall B. (2009). *Culturally proficient leadership: The personal journey begins within.* Thousand Oaks, CA: Corwin.

U.N. Human Rights Office of the High Commissioner. (2012). *Born free and equal: Sexual orientation and gender identity in international human rights law* (HR/PUB/12/06). New York, NY: United Nations.

U.S. Department of Health and Human Services. (2012a). *Components in state anti-bullying laws.* Retrieved from http://www.stopbullying.gov/laws/key-components/

U.S. Department of Health and Human Services. (2012b). *What is bullying?* Retrieved from http://www.stopbullying.gov/what-is-bullying/index.html

Vaill, Peter B. (1966). *Learning as a way of being: Strategies for survival in a world of permanent white water.* San Francisco, CA: Jossey-Bass.

Wagner, Tony, Kegan, Robert, Lahey, Lisa Laskow, Lemons, Richard W., Garnier, Jude, Helsing, Deborah, . . . Rasmussen, Harriette Thurber. (2006). *Change leadership: A practical guide to transforming our schools.* San Francisco, CA: John Wiley.

Webber, Carlisle K. (2010). *Gay, lesbian, bisexual, transgender and questioning teen literature: A guide to reading interests.* Santa Barbara, CA: Libraries Unlimited.

Wheatley, Margaret J. (2002). *Turning to one another: Simple conversations to restore hope to the future.* San Francisco: Berrett-Koehler.

Zander, Rosamund Stone, & Zander, Benjamin. (2000). *The art of possibility: Transforming professional and personal life.* New York, NY: Penguin.

Index

Aboriginal communities, 48, 49, 51
Abusive behaviors, 39
ACT (Assets Coming Together) for Youth
    Center of Excellence, 147
Action plans, 5–6, 21–22, 69, 119–120
Adapting to Diversity
    assets perspective, 103–104
    definition, 24, 29, 58, 100
    inside-out change processes, 104–105
    school community, 101
    supportive environments, 105–106
    Westfield Unified School District case
        story, 102–103
Advocacy
    see Proactive behaviors and practices
Advocates for Youth, 147
African Americans, 48
Ally involvement, 118–119
American exceptionalism, 47
Antibullying programs, 4–5, 45–47, 66–68,
    93, 95
Assessing Cultural Knowledge
    beliefs and assumptions, 79
    definition, 24, 29, 58, 72
    Westfield Unified School District case
        story, 73–79
Authentic representation, 41–43
Awareness, 119

Badgett, M. V. Lee, 42
Barriers to Cultural Proficiency, 22, 24, 25
Bartkiewicz, Mark J., 39, 40, 63, 65, 106
Bateson, Gregory, 29
Belief systems, 31–32, 79
Berdaches, 51–52
Berman, Steve, 144
Blackburn, Mollie V., 158
Bochenek, Michael, 40, 42
Boesen, Madelyn J., 39, 63, 106
    see also Kosciw, Joseph G.
Brown, A. Widney, 40, 42

Bullying
    antibullying programs, 4–5, 45–47,
        66–68, 93, 95
    causal factors, 62–63
    characteristics and occurrences, 61–62
    current research, 63–65
    systemic barriers, 39
    two-phase response, 65–70
Bystander-to-ally transition, 118–119

California Assembly Bill 9 (Seth's Law), 42
Cambron-McCabe, Nelda H.
    see Senge, Peter M.
CampbellJones, Brenda, 101, 155
CampbellJones, Franklin, 101, 153, 155
Campos, David, 5, 6, 14, 15, 16, 51,
    55, 69, 110
Canada
    human and civil rights issues,
        47–50
    protective actions, 42
    same-sex relations, 51
Candor, 98
Case studies
    see Westfield Unified School District
        case story
Center for Adaptive Schools, 148
Center for Cognitive Coaching, 148
Centering activities
    adapting to diversity, 100–101
    antibullying messages, 45–47
    bullying, 60–61
    diversity-valuing behaviors, 82
    equality versus equity, 35–36
    institutionalizing cultural knowledge,
        108–109
    managing the dynamics of difference,
        91–92
    personal reflection and organizational
        dialogue, 19–22
    sexual orientation, 9, 72–73

Centers for Disease Control and
    Prevention (CDC), 148
Chittister, Joan, 97
Civil rights, 47, 52–53
Civil Rights Act (1867), 37
Civil Rights Act (1964), 37
Clarity, 98
Clark, Caroline T., 158
Commitment to change, 27, 29–31,
    123–124
Community resources, 147–151
Compassion, 98
Conceptual framework, 22–26
Confidence, 98
Conflict management, 91–92
Continuum Concepts of Cultural
    Proficiency, 23, 26–27, 28, 69
Corbin, Linda K., 9, 51
Courage, 98
Critical conversations, 98–99, 124
Cross-cultural communication, 11–12,
    83–84
Cross, Terry L., 5, 6, 17, 25, 69
Cuéntame, 148
Cultural proficiency resources,
    140, 152–157
Culture, definition of, 14

Deal, Terrence A., 26
DeColores Queer Orange County, 149
Dei, George, 91
DeVoe, Jill, 61
DeWitt, Peter M., 55, 72, 100, 105, 110
Dialogic activities
    adapting to diversity, 107
    assessing cultural knowledge, 80–81
    authentic representation, 54–55
    bullying, 71
    diversity-valuing behaviors and
        assessments, 89–90
    equitable treatment, 44
    identity and belief systems, 34
    institutionalizing cultural knowledge, 116
    managing the dynamics of difference, 99
    nested-level change model, 34
    terminology/appropriate language, 17
Diaz, Elizabeth M., 39, 106
Diaz, Richard, 60, 127, 134, 157
Dilts, Robert, 29, 120
Directory of LGBTQ People of Color
    Organizations and Projects in the
    U.S., 151
Discrimination, 39, 42, 47–50, 52
Diversity-valuing behaviors, 82–90

Dixon, Robin, 19
Dominant cultures, 96–97
Dutton, Janis
    see Senge, Peter M.

Eisner, Elliot W., 118
Equality versus equity
    authentic representation, 41–43
    barriers, 38–39
    historical context, 36–37
    operational definitions, 37–38
    protective actions, 42–43
Essential Elements of Cultural Proficiency
    adapting to diversity, 24, 29, 58, 100–107
    antibullying programs, 69
    assessing cultural knowledge, 72–81
    characteristics, 24, 26–27, 29, 58
    diversity-valuing behaviors, 82–90
    institutionalizing cultural knowledge,
        24, 29, 58, 108–116
    managing the dynamics of difference,
        24, 29, 58, 91–99
Evans, N. J., 118, 119
Evenhandedness, 38

Facilitation skills, 98–99
Fairness, 38
Faith-based tolerance, 89
Fearfulness, 97–98
Fill-in-the-blank reform model, 30–31
Franco, Carmella S., 156
Freire, P., 130
Fullan, Michael, 26

GALE Learning Community, 149
Galloway, Mary, 146
Garmston, Robert J., 29
Garnier, Jude
    see Wagner, Tony
Gay Lesbian Straight Education Network
    (GLSEN), 39, 63, 65, 69, 149
Gays, 14
Gender identity
    authentic representation, 41–43
    barriers, 38–41
    bullying/antibullying programs, 4–5
    community resources, 147–151
    definition, 14
    equity considerations, 10–12
    historical context, 10–11
    historical perspective, 51–52
    human and civil rights issues, 47–50,
        52–53
    inclusive practices, 7–8

inside-out change processes, 5–6, 21–22, 69
invisibility, 49–50, 52, 83
myopic viewpoints, 5
protective actions, 42–43
questionnaires, 142–146
research assumptions, 2–4
terminology, 13–16, 141
theological arguments, 5
Tools of Cultural Proficiency, 16–18
Germany, 52
Graham, Stephanie M., 154
Greytak, Emily A., 39, 40, 63, 65, 106
Guckenburg, Sarah, 61
Guiding Principles of Cultural Proficiency, 22, 24, 25–26
Gutierrez, Jorge, 150

Hall, M., 159
Hanson, Thomas L., 61
Haugen, Mary Margaret, 89
Hazelden Foundation, 69
Healthy Gay, Lesbian and Bisexual Students Project, 148
Helsing, Deborah
    see Wagner, Tony
Heteronormative worldviews, 50–51
Heterosexism, 15, 51–53, 96–97, 125
Heterosexuals, 14
Homophobia, 15–16, 125
Homosexuals, 14
Human rights, 47, 52–53
Humphreys, Griff, 144

Impartiality, 38
Indentity and belief systems, 31–32
Inside-out change processes
    adapting to diversity, 104–105
    ally involvement, 118–119
    inside-out action plan, 5–6, 21–22, 69
    institutionalizing cultural knowledge, 109–112
    sexual orientation, 5–6, 21–22, 69
Institutionalizing Cultural Knowledge
    definition, 23, 29, 58, 108
    inside-out change processes, 109–112
    professional learning communities, 114–115
    Westfield Unified School District case story, 112–114
Institutional policies and practices, 84–86
Internal language, definition of, 16
Inuit, 49
Invisibility, 49–50, 52, 83

Jeppson, Jandy, 159
Jer's Vision, 2–3, 69
Jew, Cynthia L., 154
Jungwirth, Linda D., 115, 154

Karns, Michelle S., 118, 155
Kegan, Robert
    see Wagner, Tony
Kennedy, Allan A., 26
Kenney, Lauren M., 158
Kleiner, Art
    see Senge, Peter M.
Knowledge and education, 119
Kosciw, Joseph G., 39, 40, 63, 65, 106

Lahey, Lisa Laskow
    see Wagner, Tony
Latino Equality Alliance (LEA), 150
Learning Network, 150
Leaves-of-absence policies, 85
Legalized discrimination, 48–49
Lemons, Richard W.
    see Wagner, Tony
Lesbians, 14
Levels of commitment, 27, 29–31, 123–124
LGBTQ (lesbian-gay-bisexual-transgender-queer/questioning) community, 15
Lifestyle, definition of, 16
Lindsey, Delores B., 5, 19, 24, 27, 30, 33, 114, 115, 131–132, 134, 152, 153, 154, 157
Lindsey, Randall B., 5, 6, 10, 19, 24, 25, 27, 28, 29, 30, 33, 45, 101, 114, 115, 118, 125–126, 134, 152, 153, 154, 155, 156, 157
Listening skills, 85
Local education agency (LEA) policies, 67–68
Lucas, Timothy
    see Senge, Peter M.

Managing the Dynamics of Difference
    antibullying programs, 95
    definition, 23, 29, 58, 91
    facilitation skills, 98–99
    fearfulness, 97–98
    heterosexism, 96–97
    micro-aggressions/micro-assaults, 96–97
    religious beliefs, 94–95
    targets/target groups, 95–96
    Westfield Unified School District case story, 92–94
Martinez, Richard S., 19, 27, 30, 33, 153
McIntosh, Peggy, 146

Meaningful interactions, 83–84
Medieval Europe, 52
Métis, 49
Micro-aggressions/micro-assaults, 96–97
Miller, Neil, 14, 51, 52, 55
Murray, Stephen O., 5, 11, 14
Myatt, Keith, 118, 155
Myers-Walls, Judith A., 159

Name-calling, 39
National Crime Victimization Survey
    School Crime Supplement, 61–62
Native First Nations people, 48, 49, 51
Nazi Germany, 52
Nested-level change model, 29–31,
    33, 120
New Day Films, 149
Nuri-Robins, Kikanza, 5, 19, 24, 25, 114,
    128–129, 134, 152, 157

Olweus, Dan, 61
Ontario Ministry of Education, 91
Organizational culture transformations,
    26–27
Organizational dialogue, 19–22
Ostracism, 39
Ott, Maria G., 156

Pahl, Jarvis V. N. C., 115, 154
Palmer, Neal A., 39, 63, 106
    see also Kosciw, Joseph G.
Parents, Families and Friends of Lesbians
    and Gays (PFLAG), 81, 149–150
Persistence, 84
Personal reflection, 19–22, 120–122
    see also Reflective activities
Petrosino, Anthony, 61
Physical abuse, 39
Powerlessness, 40–41
Proactive behaviors and practices,
    83–86
Professional learning communities,
    114–115
Professional-related reflection, 122–123
Protective actions, 42–43

Quezada, Reyes. L., 19, 157

Racism, 48–49, 125
Rainbow Project, 147–148
Rasmussen, Harriette Thurber
    see Wagner, Tony
Reflective activities
    adapting to diversity, 103, 106–107

antibullying programs, 68
assessing cultural knowledge, 78–80
authentic representation, 54
bullying, 70–71
diversity-valuing behaviors and
    assessments, 88–89
equitable treatment, 43–44
institutionalizing cultural knowledge,
    115–116
managing the dynamics of difference, 99
personal reflection, 19–22, 120–122
professional-related reflection, 122–123
prominent LGBT people, 50
resource guide, 134–139
terminology/appropriate language,
    13, 17
Tools of Cultural Proficiency, 32
Religious beliefs, 94–95, 125
Repressive systems, 52
Respect, 83, 89
Robers, Simone, 63
Roberts, Laraine M., 153
Roberts, Terrence, 48–49
Robles, Darline P., 156
Rochlin, Martin, 144

Safe and supportive environments,
    105–106
Safe place plans, 77–78
Safe Schools Coalition, 150
Same-sex orientation
    definition, 15
    historical perspective, 51–52
Sanctioned discrimination, 47–49
Schein, Edgar, 26
Senge, Peter M., 26
Sexual harassment, 39
Sexual identity, definition of, 14
Sexual orientation
    authentic representation, 41–43
    barriers, 38–41
    bullying/antibullying programs,
        4–5
    community resources, 147–151
    definition, 14
    equity considerations, 10–12
    historical context, 10–11
    historical perspective, 51–52
    human and civil rights issues, 47–50,
        52–53
    inclusive practices, 7–8
    inside-out change processes, 5–6,
        21–22, 69
    invisibility, 49–50, 52, 83

myopic viewpoints, 5
protective actions, 42–43
questionnaires, 142–146
research assumptions, 2–4
terminology, 13–16, 141
theological arguments, 5
Tools of Cultural Proficiency,
    16–18
Sexual preference, definition of, 16
Shulman, Lee, 108
Silence, effects of, 40–41
Skills development, 119
Smith, Bryan
    see Senge, Peter M.
Smith, Jill M., 158
Sodomy laws, 52
Southern Poverty Law Center, 69
Standards
    see Essential Elements of Cultural
    Proficiency
Stephens, Diana L., 156
Student suicide, 75
Sue, Derald Wing, 96
Sullivan, Michael K., 15, 51, 55

Taboo topics, 39
Targets/target groups, 95–96
Terrell, Raymond D., 5, 6, 10, 19, 24,
    25, 28, 29, 45, 114, 130, 134, 152,
    154, 157
Theological arguments, 5
Tobias, Philip, 19
Tolerance, 83, 89
Tools of Cultural Proficiency
    advantages, 16–17, 53–54
    barriers, 22–23, 25
    conceptual framework, 22–26
    continuum concepts, 24, 26–27, 28
    essential elements, 24, 26–27, 29, 57–59
    guiding principles, 22–23, 25–26
    personal reflection and organizational
        dialogue, 19–22
    see also Essential Elements of Cultural
        Proficiency
Transgender, 15
Truman, Jennifer, 63
Two-spirit people, 51–52

U.N. Human Rights Office of the High
    Commissioner, 42, 52–53
United States
    human and civil rights issues, 47–50
    protective actions, 42
    same-sex relations, 51
Unmentionable topics, 39
U.S. Declaration of Independence, 35, 36–37
U.S. Department of Health and Human
    Services, 62, 63, 66, 68
U.S. Department of Justice, 61

Vaill, Peter B., 109
Valuing Diversity
    culturally proficient components, 82–86
    definition, 23, 29, 58
    Westfield Unified School District case
        story, 74–79, 86–88

Wagner, Tony, 26
Walsh, Seth, 42
Washington, J., 118, 119
Webber, Carlisle K., 14
Wellman, Bruce M., 29
Westfield Unified School District case
    story
    adapting to diversity, 102–103
    antibullying programs, 93
    background information, 12–13, 57–59,
        73–74
    diversity-valuing behaviors and
        assessments, 74–79, 86–88
    institutionalizing cultural knowledge,
        112–114
    managing the dynamics of difference,
        92–94
    nested-level change model, 31–32, 33
Westphal, R. Chris, Jr., 154
Wheatley, Margaret J., 1, 124
Whisper campaigns, 39
Williams, Walter, 51

xQsíMagazine, 150–151

Zander, Benjamin, 104
Zander, Rosamund Stone, 104
Zhang, Jijun, 63